Brief

Microsoft® PowerPoint® 4.0 for Windows™

BEVERLY B. ZIMMERMAN

S. SCOTT ZIMMERMAN

Brigham Young University

A Susan Solomon Book

Course Technology

Course Technology, Inc. *One Main Street, Cambridge, MA 02142*

An International Thomson Publishing Company

I(T)P

Albany • Bonn • Boston • Cincinnati • London • Madrid • Melbourne • Mexico City
New York • Paris • San Francisco • Singapore • Tokyo • Toronto • Washington

PowerPoint 4.0 for Windows — New Perspectives Brief is published by Course Technology, Inc.

Managing Editor	Mac Mendelsohn
Series Consulting Editor	Susan Solomon
Product Manager	Barbara Clemens
Production Editor	Catherine Griffin
Text Designer	Sally Steele
Cover Designer	John Gamache

For more information contact:
Course Technology, Inc.
One Main Street
Cambridge, MA 02142

International Thomson Publishing Europe
Berkshire House 168-173
High Holborn
London WCIV 7AA
England

International Thomson Publishing GmbH
Königswinterer Strasse 418
53227 Bonn
Germany

Thomas Nelson Australia
102 Dodds Street
South Melbourne, 3205
Victoria, Australia

International Thomson Publishing Asia
211 Henderson Road
#05-10 Henderson Building
Singapore 0315

Nelson Canada
1120 Birchmount Road
Scarborough, Ontario
Canada M1K 5G4

International Thomson Publishing Japan
Hirakawacho Kyowa Building, 3F
2-2-1 Hirakawacho
Chiyoda-ku, Tokyo 102
Japan

International Thomson Editores
Campos Eliseos 385, Piso 7
Col. Polanco
11560 Mexico D.F. Mexico

Trademarks

Disclaimer

ISBN 0-7600-3277-7

Printed in the United States of America

10 9 8 7 6 5 4 3 2 1

Preface

Course Technology, Inc. is proud to present this new book in its New Perspectives (formerly Windows) Series. *Microsoft PowerPoint 4.0 — New Perspectives Brief* is designed to introduce students to the essential features of Microsoft PowerPoint. This book capitalizes on the energy and enthusiasm students naturally have for Windows-based applications and clearly teaches students how to take full advantage of PowerPoint features.

Organization and Coverage

Microsoft PowerPoint 4.0 for Windows — New Perspectives Brief begins with a tour of PowerPoint's features, and then teaches students how to create their own text presentations, work with and add graphics, and present a complete slide show. Presentation planning is emphasized from the start, and Design Principle Windows throughout the text help students avoid common errors in designing presentations.

Approach

Microsoft PowerPoint 4.0 for Windows — New Perspectives Brief distinguishes itself from other Windows textbooks because of its unique two-pronged approach. First, it motivates students by demonstrating *why* they need to learn the concepts and skills. This book teaches PowerPoint using a task-driven, rather than a feature-driven approach. By working through the tutorials, students learn how to use PowerPoint in situations they are likely to encounter in the workplace, rather than learn a laundry list of features one-by-one out of context. Second, the content, organization, and pedagogy of this book make full use of the Windows environment.

Features

Microsoft PowerPoint 4.0 for Windows— New Perspectives Brief is an exceptional textbook also because it includes the following features:

- **"Read This Before You Begin" Page** This page is consistent with Course Technology's unequaled commitment to helping instructors introduce technology into the classroom. Technical considerations and assumptions about hardware, software, and default settings are listed in one place to help instructors save time and eliminate unnecessary aggravation.
- **Tutorial Case** Each Windows tutorial begins with a business-related problem that students could reasonably encounter. Thus, the process of solving the problem will be meaningful to students. These cases touch on multicultural and international issues—so important to today's business curriculum.
- **TROUBLE?** TROUBLE? paragraphs anticipate the mistakes that students are likely to make and help them recover from these mistakes. This feature facilitates independent learning and frees the instructor to focus on substantive conceptual issues rather than common procedural errors.
- **Task Reference** The Task Reference appears at the end of the book and summarizes how to accomplish tasks using the mouse, the menus, and the keyboard.
- **Questions, Tutorial Assignments, and Case Problems** Each tutorial concludes with meaningful, conceptual Questions that test students' understanding of what they learned

in the tutorial. The Questions are followed by Tutorial Assignments, which provide students with additional hands-on practice of the skills they learned in the Tutorial, and Case Problems with approximately the same scope as the Tutorial case.

- **Exploration Exercises** The Windows environment allows students to learn by exploring and discovering what they can do. The Exploration Exercises are Questions or Tutorial Assignments designated by an E that encourage students to explore the capabilities of the computing environment they are using and to extend their knowledge using the Windows on-line Help facility and other reference materials.

The CTI WinApps Setup Disk

The CTI WinApps Setup Disk, bundled with the Instructor's copy of this book, contains an innovative Student Disk generating program that is designed to save instructors time. Once this software is installed on a network or a standalone workstation, students can double click the "Make PowerPoint 4.0 Student Disks" icon in the CTI WinApps icon group. Double clicking this icon transfers all the data files students need to complete the tutorials, and Tutorial Assignments, to high-density disks in drive A or B. These files free students from tedious keystroking and allow them to concentrate on mastering the concept or task at hand.

Adopters of this text are granted the right to install the CTI WinApps icon group on any standalone computer or network used by students who have purchased this text. For more information on the CTI WinApps Setup Disk, see the page in this book called "Read This Before You Begin."

Supplements

- **Instructor's Manual** The Instructor's Manual is written by the authors and is quality assurance tested. It includes:
  - Answers and solutions to all of the Questions, Tutorial Assignments, and Case Problems. Suggested solutions are also included for the Exploration Exercises
  - A 3.5-inch disk containing solutions to all of the Questions, Tutorial Assignments, and Case Problems.
  - Tutorial Notes, which contain background information from the authors about the Tutorial Case and the instructional progression of the tutorial
  - Technical Notes, which include troubleshooting tips as well as information on how to customize the students' screens to closely emulate the screen shots in the book
  - Transparency Masters of key concepts
- **Test Bank** The Test Bank uses the **Course On-Line Test Manager**, which gives instructors unprecedented ability to give on-line tests with automatic grading. Select questions from a bank of 150 questions per tutorial include customized questions, and give pretests and practice tests. Questions can even include graphics. The Course On-Line Test Manager frees instructors to do what they do best: teach.

Acknowledgments

The authors would like to thank the following reviewers for their valuable feedback on this very exciting project: Sherri Cady, Anoka-Ramsey Community College; Emily Ketcham, Baylor University; Catherine Rathke, College of DuPage; and Linda Wise Miller, University of Idaho.

Also special thanks to: Susan Solomon, Series Consulting Editor; Mac Mendelsohn, Managing Editor; Barbara Clemens, Product Manager; Catherine Griffin, Production Editor; Jeff Goding, Editorial Services Manager; and student testers Chris Greacen, Thomas Cutter, and Christian Murphy.

Finally we would like to thank Kitty Pinard, our developmental editor, for her many excellent suggestions and her constant guidance, encouragement, and support.

Contents

TUTORIAL 2 Creating a Text Slide Show PP 26

TUTORIAL 3 Creating Graphics for Your Slides PP 53

Brief PowerPoint 4.0 for Windows Tutorials

1 A Tour of PowerPoint 4.0

2 Creating a Text Slide Show

3 Creating Graphics for Your Slides

4 Presenting a Slide Show

Read This Before You Begin

To the Student

To use this book, you must have Student Disks. Your instructor will either provide you with them or ask you to make your own by following the instructions in the section "Your Student Disks" in Tutorial 1. See your instructor or technical support person for further information. If you are going to work through this book using your own computer, you need a computer system running Microsoft Windows 3.1, Microsoft PowerPoint 4.0 for Windows, and Student Disks. *You will not be able to complete the tutorials and exercises in this book using your own computer until you have Student Disks.* You will need three blank, formatted disks. Label each with the appropriate tutorial number(s) based on the following table, which summarizes how the disk creation program will place files on your disks:

Student Disk	Tutorial(s)
1	1+2
2	3
3	4

To the Instructor

Making the Student Disks To complete the tutorials in this book, your students must have a copy of the Student Disks. To relieve you of having to make multiple Student Disks from a single master copy, we provide you with the CTI WinApps Setup Disk, which contains an automatic Student Disk generating program. Once you install the Setup Disk on a network or standalone workstation, students can easily make their own Student Disks by double-clicking the "Make PowerPoint 4.0 Student Disks" icon in the CTI WinApps icon group. Double-clicking this icon transfers all the data files students will need to complete the tutorials, Tutorial Assignments, and Case Problems to high-density disks in drive A or B. If some of your students will use their own computers to complete the tutorials and exercises in this book, they must first get the Student Disks. The section called "Your Student Disks" in Tutorial 1 provides complete instructions on how to make the Student Disks.

Installing the CTI WinApps Setup Disk To install the CTI WinApps icon group from the Setup Disk, follow the instructions on the Setup Disk label. By adopting this book, you are granted a license to install this software on any computer or computer network used by you or your students.

README File A README.TXT file located on the Setup Disk provides complete installation instructions, additional technical notes, troubleshooting advice, and tips for using the CTI WinApps software in your school's computer lab. You can view the README.TXT file using any word processor you choose.

Microsoft PowerPoint Installation

Make sure the Microsoft PowerPoint software has been installed on your computer using the complete setup option, rather than the laptop or typical installation.

System Requirements

The minimum software and hardware requirements for your computer system are as follows:

- Microsoft Windows Version 3.1 or later on a local hard drive or a network drive.
- A 386 or higher processor with a minimum of 4 MB RAM (486 and 8 MB recommended)
- A mouse supported by Windows 3.1.
- A printer supported by Windows 3.1.
- A VGA 64 × 480 16-color display is recommended; an 800 × 600 or 1024 × 768 SVGA, VGA monochrome, or EGA display is acceptable.
- A typical installation requires 22 MB free hard disk space, and a full installation requires 23 MB.
- Student workstations with at least 1 high-density disk drive.
- If you want to install the CTI WinApps Setup Disk on a network drive, your network must support Microsoft Windows.

TUTORIAL 1

A Tour of PowerPoint 4.0

OBJECTIVES

In this tutorial you will:

- Launch PowerPoint
- Use PowerPoint toolbars
- Plan a slide show
- Open a presentation
- Save a presentation
- View a presentation in various ways
- Print a presentation
- Use PowerPoint's on-line help
- Exit PowerPoint

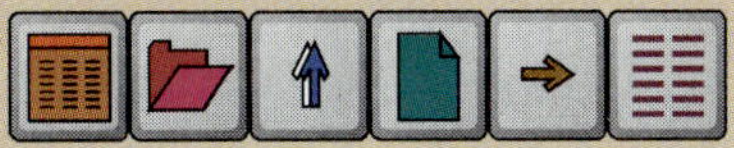

CASE **Inca Imports International** Patricia Cuevas immigrated to the United States of America from San Salvador at the age of 12. After graduating from high school, she began working for Cisco Foods, a distributor to food-services businesses in the Los Angeles area. In the evenings, Patricia attended California State University at Northridge, where she earned a degree in Business Management. After ten years with Cisco Foods, Patricia and another Cisco employee, Angelena Cristenas, began their own small business, Inca Imports International. Working with suppliers in South America, particularly in Ecuador and Peru, Patricia and Angelena imported fresh fruits and vegetables during the winter and spring in North America (which are summer and fall in South America) and sold them to small grocery stores in the Los Angeles area.

After three years in business, Inca Imports International has 34 employees and is healthy and growing. To promote further growth and profits, Patricia wants to establish a permanent distribution facility in Quito, Ecuador. This distribution facility, to include office and warehouse space, would allow Inca Imports International to maintain better quality control, shorten the time to market of the imported fruits and vegetables, and reduce costs.

As one of only three suppliers of imported fruits and vegetables in the entire Southern California area, Inca Imports International is in a position to increase the number and size of the grocery stores and restaurant chains that purchase its goods. Besides building the facility in Ecuador, Patricia plans an aggressive marketing program that would significantly increase the cash flow and value of the rapidly growing company.

In an effort to obtain funding for the new distribution facility and marketing campaign, Patricia has prepared a presentation that introduces Inca Imports International to potential investors. In this tutorial you will see the first few slides of her presentation.

Using the Tutorials Effectively

These tutorials are designed to be used at your computer. Begin by reading the text that explains the concepts. When you come to the numbered steps, read each step completely before you perform it on your computer.

As you work, compare your computer screen with the tutorial figures. The important parts of the screen display are labeled in each figure; make sure these parts match. If you have a problem, follow the procedures in the TROUBLE? paragraph that may follow a step; these paragraphs identify common problems and explain how to get back on track. Reference Windows, located throughout the tutorials, and the Task Reference, at the end of each tutorial, provide you with short summaries of frequently used procedures.

Before you begin the tutorials, you should know how to use the menus, dialog boxes, Help facility, Program Manager, and File Manager in Microsoft Windows. Course Technology, Inc. publishes two excellent texts for learning Windows: *A Guide to Microsoft Windows 3.1* and *An Introduction to Microsoft Windows 3.1*.

Your Student Disks

To complete the tutorials and exercises in this book, you must have Student Disks. The Student Disks contain all of the practice files you need for the tutorials, the Tutorial Assignments, and the Case Problems. If your instructor or technical support person provides you with Student Disks, you can skip this section and go to the section titled "What is PowerPoint?" If your instructor asks you to make your own Student Disks, follow the steps in this section.

To make your Student Disks you will need:

- Blank, formatted, high-density 3.5-inch disks. See the table on the "Read This Before You Begin" page, just before Tutorial 1, for information on the number of disks you'll need, and how to label each one.
- A computer with Microsoft Windows 3.1, PowerPoint 4.0 for Windows, and the CTI WinApps icon group installed on it.

If you're using your own computer, the CTI WinApps icon group will not be installed on it. Before you proceed, you must go to your school's computer lab and find a computer that has the CTI WinApps icon group installed. Once you have made your own Student Disks, you can use them to complete all the tutorials and exercises in this book on any computer you choose.

To make your PowerPoint Student Disks:

1. Launch Windows and make sure the Program Manager window is open.

   TROUBLE? The exact steps you follow to launch Microsoft Windows 3.1 might vary depending on how your computer is set up. On many computer systems, you must type WIN, then press [Enter] to launch Windows. If you don't know how to launch Windows, ask your instructor or technical support person.

2. Place your formatted disk for Tutorials 1–2 in drive A.

TROUBLE? If your computer has more than one disk drive, drive A is usually on top. If your Student Disk doesn't fit into drive A, then place it in drive B and substitute "drive B" anywhere you see "drive A" in the tutorial steps.

❸ Look for an icon labeled "CTI WinApps," like the one in Figure 1-1, or a window labeled "CTI WinApps," like the one in Figure 1-2.

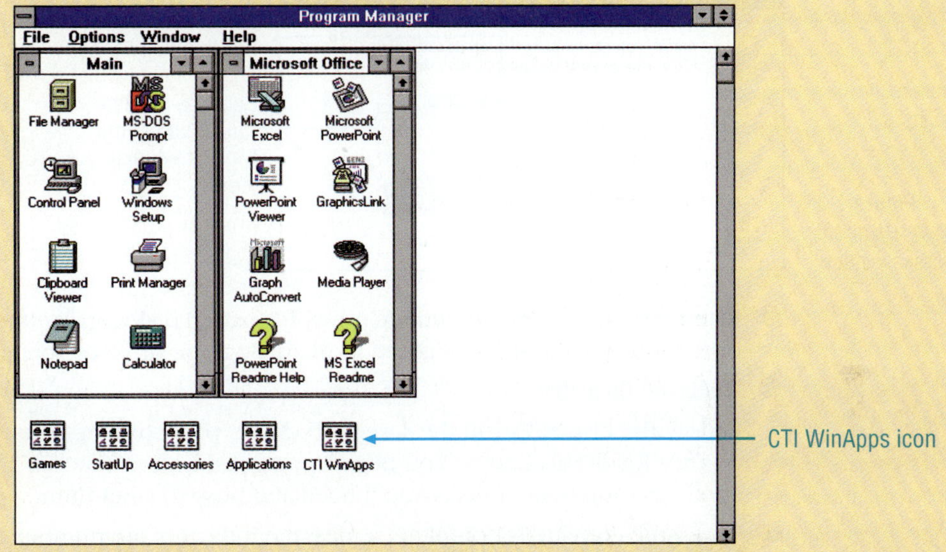

Figure 1-1
CTI WinApps icon

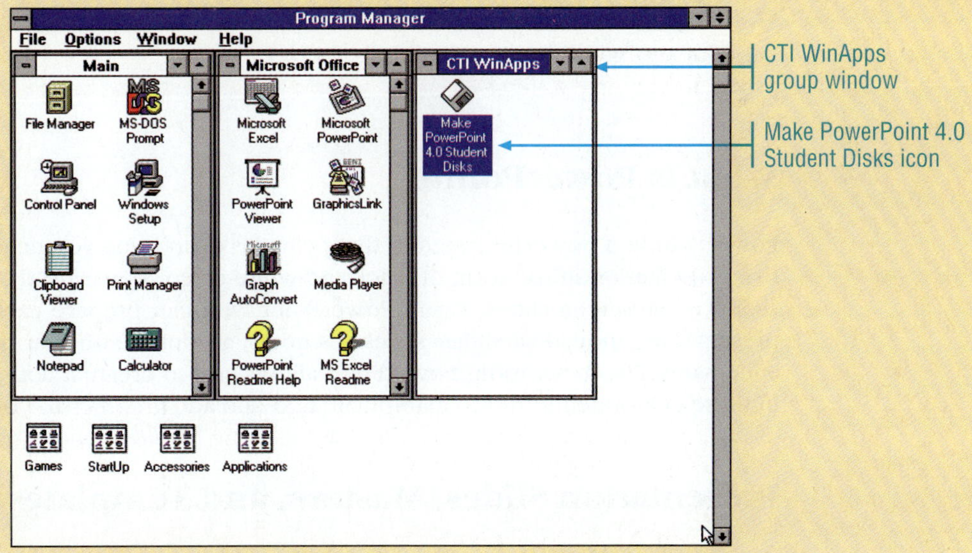

Figure 1-2
Make PowerPoint 4.0 Student Disks icon

TROUBLE? If you can't find anything labeled "CTI WinApps," the CTI software might not be installed on your computer. Ask your instructor or technical support person for assistance.

If you're using your own computer, you won't be able to make your Student Disks. To make them you need to access the CTI WinApps icon group, which is, most likely, installed on your school's lab computers. Ask your instructor or technical support person for further information on where to locate the CTI WinApps icon group. Once you create your Student Disks, you can use them to complete all the tutorials and exercises in this book on any computer you choose.

4. If you see an icon labeled "CTI WinApps," double-click it to open the CTI WinApps group window. If the CTI WinApps window is already open, proceed to Step 5.
5. Double-click the icon labeled "**Make PowerPoint 4.0 Student Disks**." The Make PowerPoint 4.0 Student Disks window opens. See Figure 1-3.

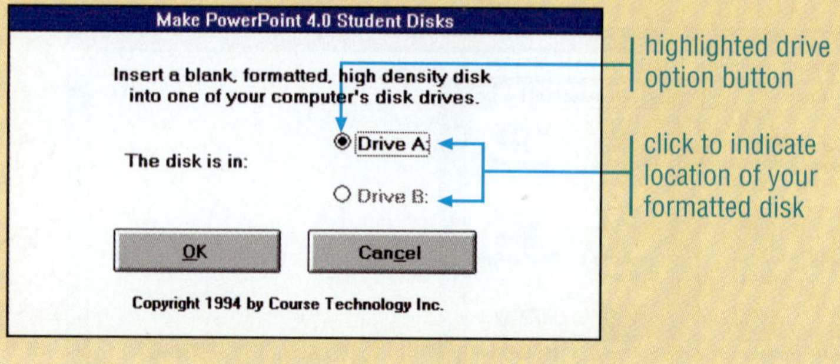

Figure 1-3
Make PowerPoint 4.0 Student Disks window

6. Make sure the drive that contains your formatted disk corresponds to the drive option button that is highlighted in the dialog box on your screen.
7. Click the **OK button**.

   Follow the directions on the screen to create your student disks. Refer to the table on the "Read This Before You Begin" page, just before Tutorial 1, for information about the numbers of disks you'll need and how to label them.
8. When the copying is complete, a message indicates the number of files copied to each disk. Click the **OK button**.
9. To close the CTI WinApps window, double-click the **Control menu box** on the CTI WinApps window.

What Is PowerPoint?

PowerPoint is a powerful program that provides everything you need to produce an effective presentation in the form of black-and-white or color overheads, 35-mm photographic slides, or on-screen slides. Using PowerPoint, you can prepare each component of your presentation: individual slides, speaker's notes, an outline of your presentation, and audience handouts. In addition, PowerPoint allows you to create a consistent format for each of these components, and to manipulate text and add graphics to your presentations.

Presentation Slides, Masters, and Templates

Before you begin this tutorial, you need to understand several key PowerPoint terms: presentation, slide, master, and template. A **presentation** is a collection of slides, handouts, speaker's notes, and an outline, all together in one file. A **slide** is a single image or picture that is part of the your visual presentation. Your presentation could include from one to dozens of slides. A **master** is a slide that contains the text and graphics that will appear on every slide in the presentation. For example, the company name, the date, and graphics such as the company logo can be put on a master so that this information will appear on every slide in the presentation. Using a master allows you to create a consistent overall format for your presentation. A **template** is a predefined format and color scheme provided in PowerPoint that you can apply to your presentation slides. PowerPoint supplies a variety of professionally designed templates.

Planning a Presentation

Planning a presentation before you create it improves the quality of your presentation, makes your presentation more effective and enjoyable, and, in the long run, saves you time and effort. As you plan your presentation, you should answer several questions. What is my purpose or objective for this presentation? What type of presentation is needed? Who is the audience? What is the physical location of my presentation? What information does that audience need? What is the best format for presenting the information contained in this presentation given the presentation location?

In planning her presentation, Patricia Cuevas answered these questions as follows:

- **Purpose for presentation:** To obtain funding
- **Type of presentation:** Sales presentation to sell expansion and marketing campaign ideas
- **Audience:** Potential investors, in their monthly board meeting or in a specially arranged meeting
- **Audience needs:** Company mission, profitability, and growth potential
- **Location of presentation:** A small boardroom with a computer and color monitor and a projection system
- **Format:** Electronic slide show consisting of 7–10 slides and speaker's notes

Having planned her presentation, Patricia used PowerPoint to create it. Let's launch PowerPoint and look at the first few slides of Patricia's presentation.

Launching PowerPoint

To use PowerPoint, you have to start (launch) the PowerPoint program. Let's do that now.

To launch PowerPoint:

❶ Make sure you have your formatted PowerPoint Student Disk.

TROUBLE? If don't have a Student Disk, you need to get one. Your instructor will either give you one or ask you to make your own by following the steps outlined earlier in this tutorial in the section called "Your Student Disk."

❷ If necessary, turn on your computer and start Windows.

The Windows Program Manager should appear on the screen. If it doesn't, consult your instructor or technical support person. Program group windows and group icons appear in the Program Manager window.

The PowerPoint icons appear in the Microsoft Office group window, as shown in Figure 1-4, or in some other window, such as the PowerPoint group window. The arrangement of windows and icons on your computer screen might be different than the one shown in Figure 1-4.

Figure 1-4 Microsoft PowerPoint icon

TROUBLE? If the PowerPoint or Microsoft Office group window does not appear on the screen, open it by double-clicking the PowerPoint or Microsoft Office group icon. If you can't locate these program groups or if the PowerPoint icon doesn't appear in the window, consult with your instructor or technical support person.

❸ Double-click the **Microsoft PowerPoint icon.**

TROUBLE? On some computers, the PowerPoint icon may be labeled "PowerPoint 4.0." Double-click that icon to launch PowerPoint.

After a moment or two, the PowerPoint startup dialog box appears on the screen. See Figure 1-5. PowerPoint is now running and ready to use.

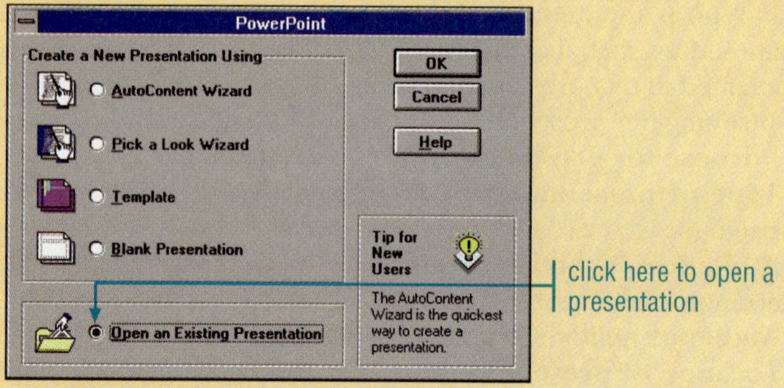

Figure 1-5
PowerPoint startup dialog box

TROUBLE? A "Tip of the Day" dialog box may first appear in the PowerPoint window. If it does, click the OK button. A dialog box asking if you want to run the PowerPoint Quick Preview may also appear. If it does, click the No or Close button.

Opening an Existing Presentation

When you launch PowerPoint, a startup dialog box appears on the screen. This dialog box contains several options. For example, it allows you to create a new presentation or to open an existing one.

REFERENCE WINDOW

Opening an Existing Presentation

- If you have just launched PowerPoint, click the Open an Existing Presentation button in the PowerPoint startup dialog box, then click the OK button or press [Enter].

or

- If PowerPoint is already running, click the Open button on the Standard toolbar, or click File, then click Open.
- From the Open dialog box, choose the disk and directory where the presentation file is located.
- Scroll through the Files list box, and click the filename of the presentation to select it.
- Click the OK button or press [Enter].

Let's open the presentation that Patricia Cuevas created for Inca Imports International.

To open Patricia's presentation:

❶ Click the **Open an Existing Presentation button** in the PowerPoint startup dialog box, then click the **OK button**. PowerPoint displays the Open dialog box. See Figure 1-6.

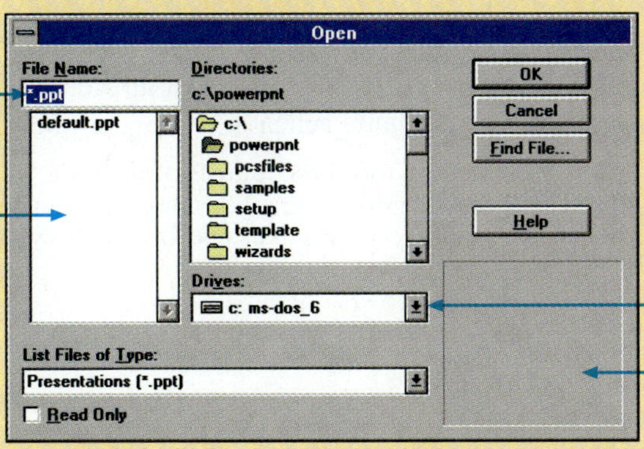

Figure 1-6
Open dialog box

❷ Click the **Down Arrow** to the right of the Drives box, and click **a:** to choose drive A (or click the drive that your Student Disk is in). The list of files on the Student Disk appears in the Files list box.

TROUBLE? If you don't see any files on the disk in drive A or if you get some other error, check to make sure that your Student Disk is in drive A. If you are using drive B, go back to Step 2 and select "b:" instead of "a:".

❸ Click the name of the presentation file **c1file1.ppt** in the Files list box. The name of the document appears in the File Name text box, and the first slide of the selected presentation file appears in the preview box in the lower-right corner of the dialog box.

❹ Click the **OK button** or press **[Enter]**.

You can press [Enter] to execute a command in a dialog box that has a dark border around it. PowerPoint opens the presentation from the disk into the PowerPoint window. See Figure 1-7.

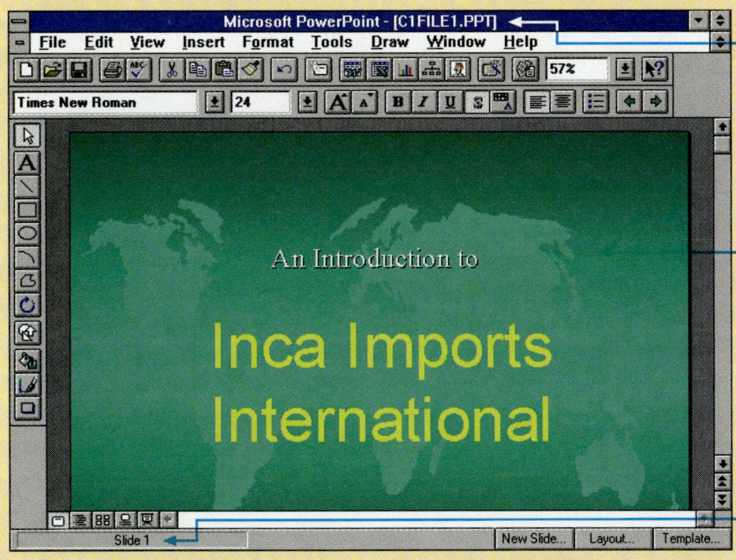

Figure 1-7
PowerPoint window after you open the presentation

TROUBLE? If the presentation window contains text in an outline format instead of the image shown in the presentation window in Figure 1-7, click View on the menu bar near the top of the screen, and then click Slides.

5. If the PowerPoint application window doesn't fill the entire monitor display, click the **Maximize button** in the upper-right corner of the PowerPoint window.
6. If the filename appears in its own title bar instead of in the application title bar as shown in Figure 1-7, click the **Maximize button** in the presentation window.

TROUBLE? Figure 1-7 shows only the top three-fourths of the slide, but your screen could show more or less than this, depending on the graphics mode of your computer system. If the area within your presentation window isn't the same as that shown in Figure 1-7, don't be concerned.

Saving the Presentation with a New Name

To avoid the problem of accidentally overwriting the original disk file C1FILE1.PPT, let's save the document using another filename. Saving the document with another filename creates a copy of the file that you can work with, leaving the original file unchanged.

To save the presentation with a new name:

1. Click **File** on the Menu bar, then click **Save As**. The Save As dialog box appears on the screen with the current filename highlighted in the File Name text box.
2. Type the new filename **s1file1** and press **[Enter]** or click the **OK button**.

   (PowerPoint automatically adds the extension .PPT. You'll learn the convention used in this book for naming files in the next tutorial.) The Save As dialog box closes and the Summary Info dialog box opens. As you create more files with PowerPoint, you will probably decide to use the Summary Info box to help you organize your files. For now, just click the OK button to close this dialog box.
3. Click the **OK button**. The Summary Info dialog box closes and the new filename is displayed in the title bar at the top of the window.

   Slide 1 of Patricia's presentation is displayed in the presentation window.

The PowerPoint Window

Let's examine the PowerPoint window, as shown in Figure 1-8. The PowerPoint window contains features common to all Windows applications, as well as features particular only to PowerPoint.

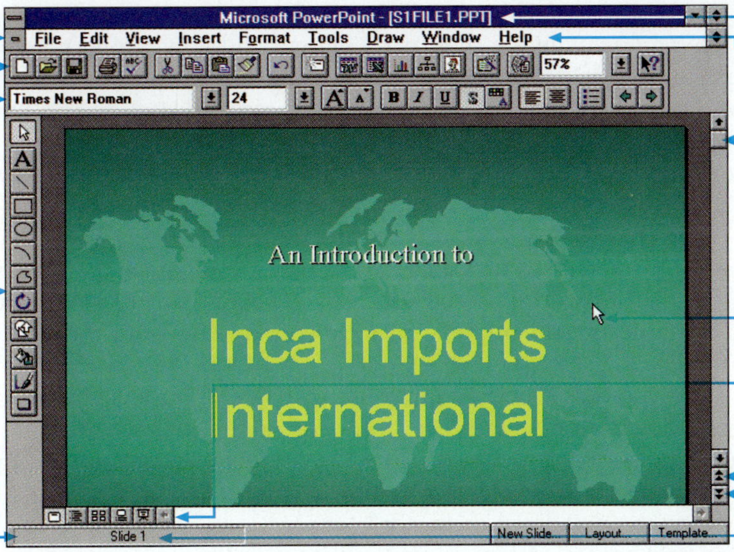

Figure 1-8 Features of PowerPoint window

Common Windows Features

Several features of the PowerPoint window are common to other Windows applications. For example, the application Control menu box allows you to minimize, maximize, and restore the PowerPoint window, to close the PowerPoint window, or to switch to another application running under Windows. In addition, the Minimize, Maximize, and Restore buttons, and the presentation Control menu box function in PowerPoint the same way they do in other Windows applications.

Scroll Bars

In PowerPoint, the vertical and horizontal scroll bars function the same way they do in other Windows applications. The scroll box in the vertical scroll bar is called the **elevator**. At the bottom of the vertical scroll bar are the Previous Slide and Next Slide buttons. Clicking these moves you to the previous or the next slide.

The Status Bar

The bottom line of the screen is called the **status bar**. It tells you which slide you're working on and, when you move the mouse pointer to a command button, provides a description of the command. The status bar also contains three shortcut buttons: the New Slide button, the Layout button, and the Template button. You will use these buttons in later tutorials.

The Toolbars

Like many Windows applications, PowerPoint supplies several toolbars, as shown in Figure 1-8. A **toolbar** is a ribbon of icons that provide menu shortcuts. When you move the mouse pointer over one of the buttons on the toolbar, the **ToolTip** for that button, a yellow square containing the name of the button, appears.

The toolbar immediately below the menu bar is the **Standard toolbar**, which you'll use to select many of the standard Windows and PowerPoint commands, such as opening an existing presentation, saving your current presentation to disk, printing the presentation, and cutting and pasting text and graphics. Below the Standard toolbar is the **Formatting toolbar**, which you'll use to format the text of your presentations. The vertical toolbar on the left edge of the PowerPoint window is the **Drawing toolbar**, which you'll use to draw lines and shapes and enter text on your slides.

Using the Toolbars feature on the View menu, you can turn ToolTips off, display other toolbars such as an additional drawing toolbar or the Microsoft toolbar, hide the toolbars that PowerPoint automatically displays, or create a customized toolbar. You can also hide or add buttons on a toolbar by choosing the Customize feature on the Tools menu.

As with other Windows applications, PowerPoint lets you select commands by using the pull-down menus with the keyboard or the mouse, by using shortcut keys, or by using buttons on a toolbar. Because the buttons on the toolbars are usually the simplest and fastest method of selecting commands, in these tutorials you'll use the toolbars more often than the pull-down menus or keyboard.

The View Toolbar

The small toolbar immediately above the status bar is the **View toolbar**, which contains buttons that allow you to change the way you view a slide presentation. Each way of seeing a presentation is called a **view**. The status bar indicates which view you are in. Clicking the **Slide View button** allows you to see and edit text and graphics on an individual slide. You are in Slide view now. You click the **Outline View button** to see and edit your entire presentation in outline format. Clicking the **Slide Sorter View button** changes the view to miniature images of all the slides at once. You use this view to change the order of the slides or set special features for your slide show. Clicking the **Notes Pages View button** changes the view so that you can see and edit your presentation notes on individual slides. To actually present your slide show, you click the **Slide Show button**. You can also change views by clicking View on the menu bar, then selecting the view you want.

Previewing the Presentation and Changing the Slide Order

Patricia wants to see all of her slides at once to check the order of the slides. Let's use the View toolbar to switch to Slide Sorter view to preview all of Patricia's slides on one screen, and then use the Slide Sorter to change the order of the slides.

To view a slide show in Slide Sorter view:

1. Move the mouse pointer to the **Slide Sorter View button** on the View toolbar, but do not yet click on the mouse button. After a second or two, the ToolTip for this button appears.
2. Click .

Your screen now looks similar to Figure 1-9.

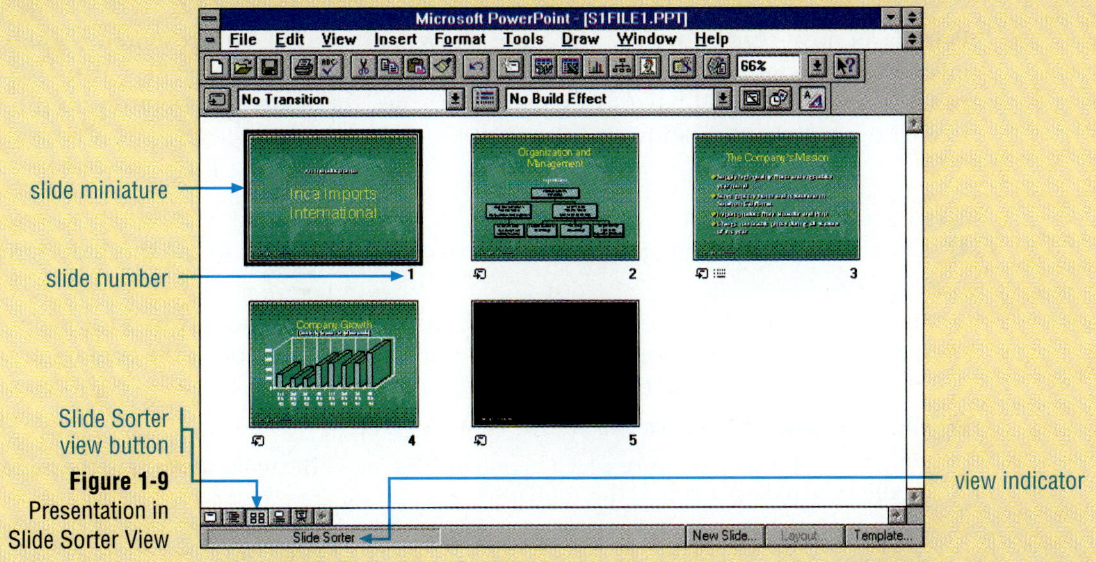

Figure 1-9
Presentation in Slide Sorter View

As you can see, each slide is shown in miniature. In the upper-left corner of the presentation window, you can see slide 1, the title slide of Patricia's presentation. To the right is slide 2, which shows the company management personnel and organizational chart. Slide 3 gives the mission statement of Inca Imports International. Slide 4 presents the company's gross income by quarter over a two-year period. Slide 5 is blank, to mark the end of the slide show. So far Patricia has made only these five slides.

At this point Patricia realizes that slide 3 (company's mission statement) should go before slide 2 (organization and management chart). Let's use the Slide Sorter View to change the order of her slides.

To change the order of the slides:

❶ Click slide 3. A heavy black line appears around slide 3 to show that it is selected.

❷ Drag the mouse pointer between slides 1 and 2, but do not release the mouse button. The mouse pointer changes to . A dotted horizontal line with an arrow at either end shows the slide's new position.

❸ Release the mouse button. The mission statement slide becomes slide 2 and the organizational chart slide becomes slide 3.

Viewing the Slide Show

Patricia is now ready to view the slide show as it would be presented to potential investors. Although the presentation you're looking at has only five slides, Patricia's completed presentation will have many more. Let's use the Slide Show button on the View toolbar to view the slide show.

To view the slide show:

1. Click slide 1 in the Slide Sorter view to make the first slide active in the Slide Sorter window.

   When you run a slide show, the first slide that appears on the screen is the slide that is selected; therefore, if you want to start the presentation at the beginning you have to select slide 1.

2. Click the **Slide Show button** on the View toolbar.

   TROUBLE? If you're not sure which button to click, move the mouse pointer to the buttons on the View toolbar and read the ToolTips.

   The first slide fills the entire screen. See Figure 1-10. Notice the company name in the lower-left corner. This text is on the master slide and will appear on every slide in the presentation. To advance to the next slide, click the left mouse button or press [Spacebar]. To go back to the previous slide, click the right mouse button or press [←]. After looking over slide 1, Patricia is ready to advance to slide 2.

text on master slide appears on every slide

slide number (changes to pencil if you move mouse)

Figure 1-10 Slide 1 of presentation

3. Click the left mouse button or press **[Spacebar]**. Don't worry about the location of the mouse pointer.

   PowerPoint advances from slide 1 to slide 2. This new slide displays only the title "The Company's Mission," not the actual text of the mission. This is because Patricia made this a build slide. A **build slide** is a slide in which a list builds one point at a time as you click the left mouse button or press [Spacebar].

❹ Click the left mouse button or press **[Spacebar]**.

The first item in the bulleted list, "Supply high-quality fruits and vegetables year round," appears on the slide. Patricia has used a build effect called **fly from right**, which, as you can see, causes the item to appear on the screen moving right to left.

❺ Click the left mouse button or press **[Spacebar]**.

Notice that the first item in the list changes color and the second item, "Serve grocery stores and restaurants in Southern California" flies onto the screen. See Figure 1-11.

Figure 1-11 Slide 2 of presentation

❻ Click the left mouse button twice or press **[Spacebar]** twice, so that the last two items in the list of the company's mission appear on the screen. You're now ready to advance the presentation to slide 3.

❼ Click the left mouse button or press **[Spacebar]**.

PowerPoint now displays the organization and management chart of Inca Imports International. This organizational chart was created using Microsoft Organization Chart, a separate applications program that ships with PowerPoint.

❽ Click the left mouse button or press **[Spacebar]**.

PowerPoint displays slide 4, which is a chart showing Inca Imports' gross income over a two-year period. See Figure 1-12. Patricia created this chart by typing numbers into a table and then letting PowerPoint do the work of formatting and displaying the information in an attractive three-dimensional graph.

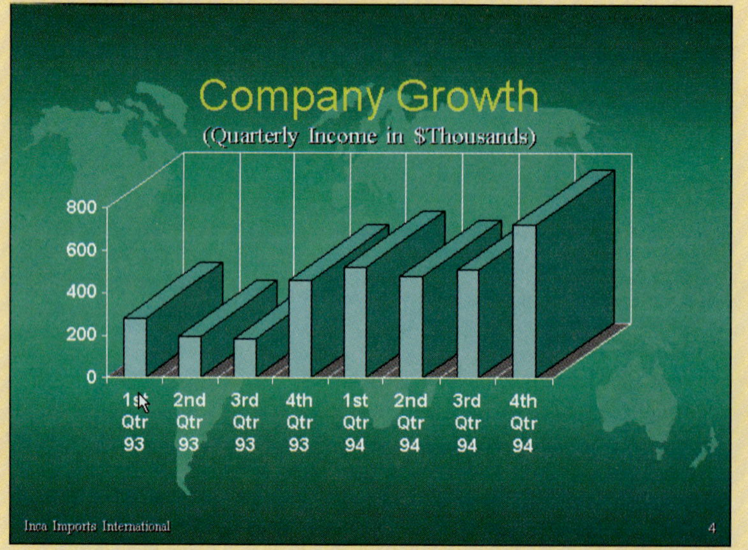

Figure 1-12 Slide 4 of presentation

❾ Click the left mouse button twice or press **[Spacebar]** twice, once to display the blank slide that tells Patricia she's at the end of her presentation, and a second time to return to the Slide Sorter view of PowerPoint.

As you can see, Patricia has created an attractive, effective slide presentation. PowerPoint has many features that allow you to create presentations like this one with a minimum of work and a maximum of efficiency.

Viewing the Outline and Speaker's Notes

A presentation includes much more than just slides. It can also include an outline, speaker's notes, and handouts. Let's view the presentation outline and speaker's notes. (**Handouts** are simply printouts of the slides, with two, three, or six slides printed on each page.)

To view the presentation Outline and the Speaker's Notes:

❶ Click the **Outline View button** on the View toolbar.

PowerPoint displays the outline of the presentation and the Outlining toolbar appears. See Figure 1-13.

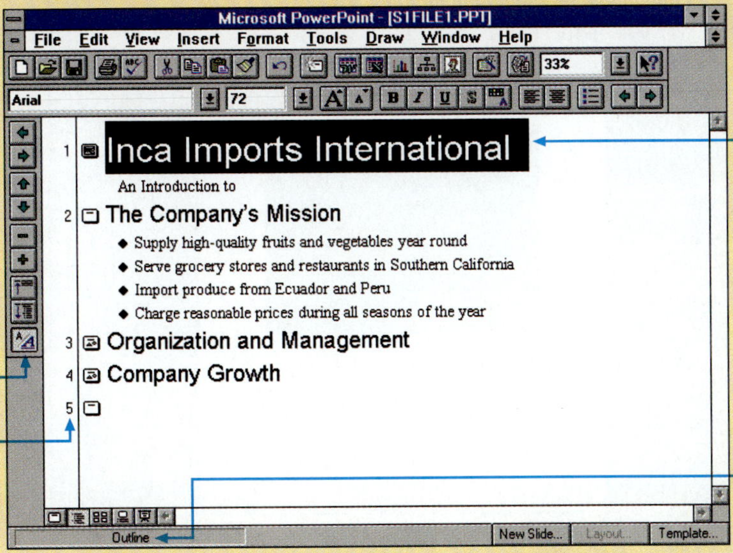

Figure 1-13
Presentation in Outline View

With the outline on the screen, you can edit the text of the slides, just as you would edit text with a word processor. The changes you make to the outline will automatically appear on the slide images. In later tutorials, you'll use Outline View to create text for your slides.

❷ Click the **Note Pages View button** .

PowerPoint displays a note page, which includes a copy of the slide at the top of the page and space for speaker's notes at the bottom of the page. The page is displayed 100% of its size. Let's set the page zoom to 50% so that we can see the entire notes page on the screen at once.

❸ Click **View**, click **Zoom**, then click the **50% button** in the Zoom dialog box, and click the **OK button**.

You should be viewing the notes for slide 1. See Figure 1-14. If you don't see the full slide at the top of the page, drag the elevator up to the top of the scroll bar. If you can't read the text of the speaker's notes, use the Zoom command (as you did in Step 3 above) to increase the zoom to 100%. After you read the notes for slide 1, you are ready to go on to slide 2. Let's use the elevator to select slide 2.

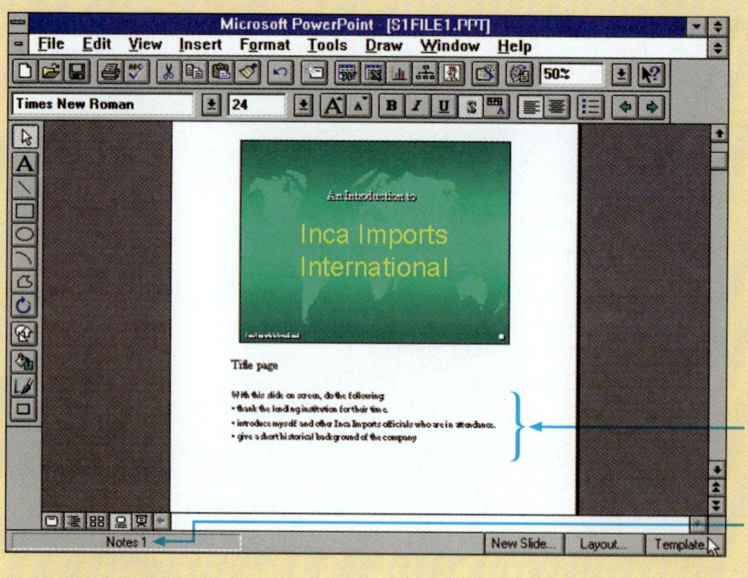

Figure 1-14 Presentation in Notes View with speaker's notes

❹ Drag the **elevator** about a third of the way down the scroll bar, but do not release the mouse button.

As you drag the elevator, PowerPoint displays the current notes number (corresponding to the slide number) next to the mouse pointer on the scroll bar. See Figure 1-15.

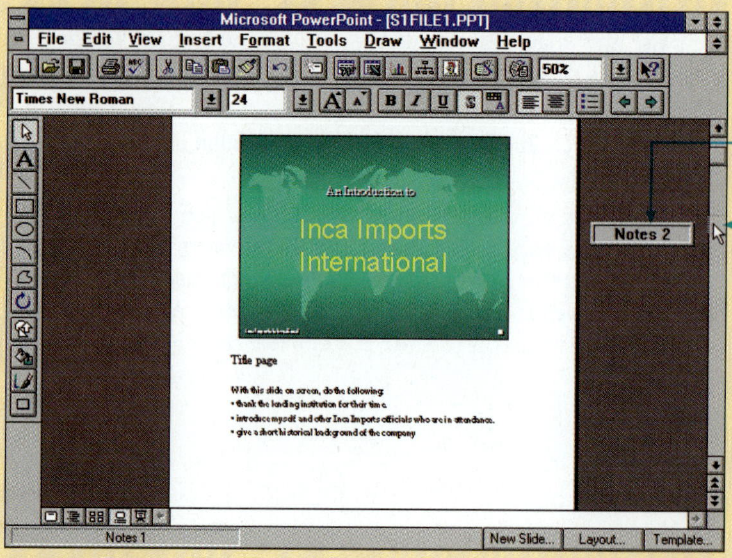

Figure 1-15 Scrolling down to notes for slide 2

❺ Release the mouse button when the elevator reaches "Notes 2."

❻ Click the **Next Slide button** at the bottom of the vertical scroll bar. PowerPoint displays slide 3.

❼ Continue going through the slides, one at a time, reading the speaker's notes.

In a later tutorial you'll learn how to create, edit, and print the speaker's notes.

Saving the Modified Presentation

Having changed the order of the slides and viewed the presentation (slides, outline, and speaker's notes), Patricia is satisfied with the results for now and decides to save the presentation to her disk. She will add more slides at another time. You must remember to save a presentation after you complete it, even if you've saved it one or more times while you were creating it. It's also a good idea to save your presentation before printing it. Let's save the presentation now.

To save a presentation to your disk:

❶ Make sure the Student Disk is still in drive A.

❷ Click the **Save button** on the Standard toolbar.

PowerPoint automatically saves the presentation using the current filename, S1FILE1.PPT.

The new version of the presentation is saved to the Student Disk in drive A.

Printing the Presentation

Patricia decides that she will print her presentation and keep the hard copy for her records. Let's do that now.

To print the presentation:

❶ Click **File**, then click **Print**. PowerPoint displays the Print dialog box. See Figure 1-16.

click to print only specified slides

click here for black-and-white printer

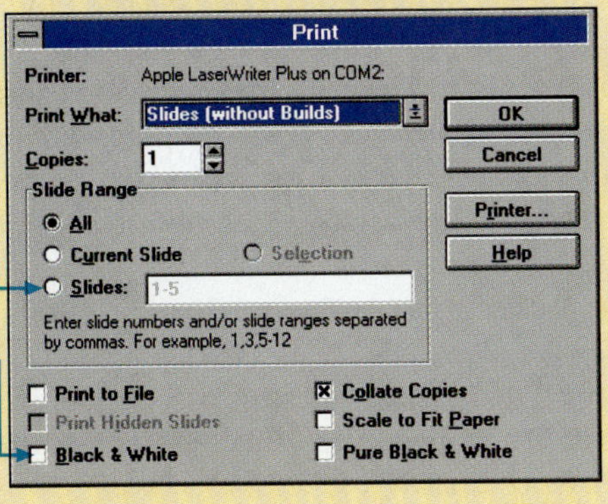

Figure 1-16
Print dialog box

To print the slides, you can be in any view except Slide Show View.

❷ Make sure **Slides (without Builds)** is selected in the Print What box.

Patricia doesn't need the blank slide at the end of the presentation printed.

❸ Click the **Slides button** in the Slide Range section of the dialog box, then press **[Del]** three times to delete the information in the Slides text box.

❹ Type **1-4** in the Slides text box to print only slides 1 throught 4.

❺ If you're using a black-and-white printer, click the **Black & White checkbox** at the lower-left of the dialog box.

❻ Click the **OK button** to print the slides.

Be patient. Graphics usually take a long time to print, even on a relatively fast laser printer. The slides are printed one slide per page. Patricia also wants to print the outline.

7. Click **File**, then click **Print**.
8. Click the **Down arrow** in the Print What text box, click **Outline View**, then click the **OK button**.

   Patricia now wants to print her speaker's notes.
9. Repeat Steps 6 and 7, only this time select **Notes Pages** in the Print What text box.

   If you click the Print button on the Standard toolbar, the presentation is printed in whatever view you are in.

Patricia now has a hard copy of her presentation.

Getting Help

When you're using PowerPoint, how do you know which button to click or which menu item to select? The best way is through training and continued experience in using PowerPoint. These tutorials will give you the training and the experience you need to perform the most important PowerPoint operations.

When you need to know something that you didn't learn in your training, PowerPoint provides two ways for you to learn which commands are available and how to execute them: the Help and Wizard features. Let's review some aspects of the Help feature. (We'll discuss the Wizard feature in the next tutorial.)

After you click Help on the menu bar, you can choose several ways of accessing the Help information. If you click Contents, PowerPoint displays the PowerPoint Help Contents window. In the Help Contents window, you can click on the green underlined text or any of the three icons to get information about PowerPoint commands and features:

- Clicking or clicking **Using PowerPoint** displays an on-line version of the printed *PowerPoint User's Guide* that comes with each PowerPoint software package. This choice lets you view step-by-step instructions on how to complete your tasks in PowerPoint.
- Clicking or clicking **Reference Information** provides definitions, descriptions, and tips on using PowerPoint.
- Clicking or clicking **Technical Reference** provides an explanation of Microsoft's support services and describes the technical support available to help you get the most from PowerPoint.

The PowerPoint Help feature also lets you search for specific information by using the "Search for Help on" command. As an example, let's use this command to get help on making an organizational chart.

REFERENCE WINDOW

Searching for Help

- Click Help on the Menu bar, then click Search for Help on.
- Type the word or phrase of the topic on which you want help.
- With the desired topic highlighted, click the Show Topics button.
- Click the desired topic to highlight it.
- Click the Go to button to display the help window on the selected topic.

To search for help on a specific topic:

1. Click **Help** on the Menu bar, then click **Search for Help on**.

   PowerPoint displays the Search dialog box. See Figure 1-17.

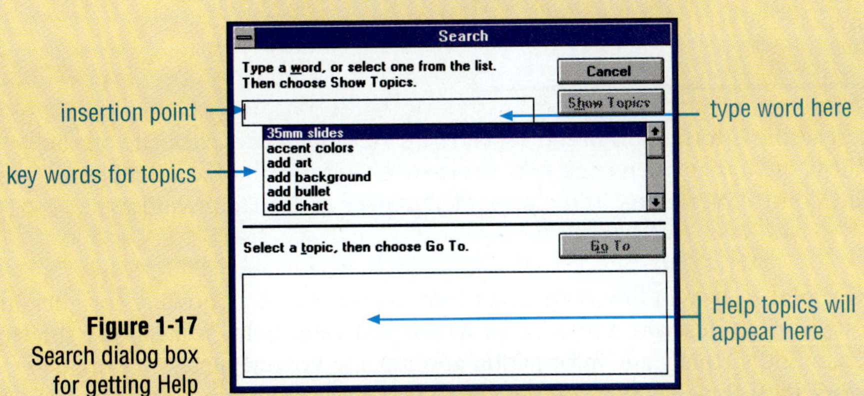

Figure 1-17
Search dialog box for getting Help

2. With the cursor in the text box at the top of the Search dialog box, type **organiz**, the first few letters of "organizational chart," the topic on which you want help.

   Notice that "organizational chart" becomes highlighted in the list of topics.

3. Click the **Show Topics button** in the Search dialog box.

   Now PowerPoint displays a list of Help topics associated with organizational charts.

4. In the list at the bottom of the dialog box, click **Creating an organizational chart** and then click the **Go To button** to tell Help to show that topic.

The screen now displays a window that describes how to create an organizational chart. See Figure 1-18.

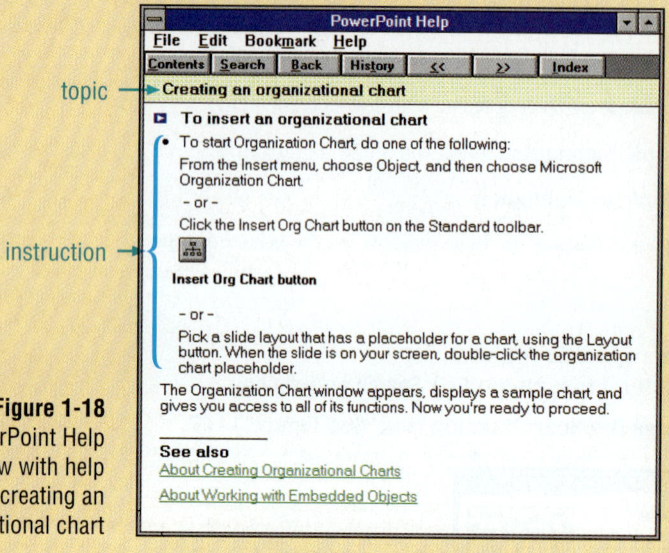

Figure 1-18 PowerPoint Help window with help on creating an organizational chart

❺ After you read the information in the PowerPoint Help window, click **File** on the Help window menu bar, then click **Exit**. Alternatively, you could have double-clicked the Control menu box in the upper-left corner of the Help window.

The PowerPoint Help window disappears from the screen. By knowing (or guessing) one or more words that describe a feature on which you want help, you can use the Help Search feature to find virtually any information about using PowerPoint.

As you work with PowerPoint, you'll want to use other methods for getting help. To access context-sensitive Help, that is, Help about a specific part of the PowerPoint window, use the Help button on the Standard toolbar. When you click that button and then click any feature within the PowerPoint window or click a pull-down menu command, PowerPoint gives you help on the feature or command. You can also use Cue Cards, an on-line coach that walks you through a step-by-step procedure to accomplish tasks in PowerPoint. The Cue Cards feature is on the Help menu on the menu bar. There are other methods for getting help on the Help menu. Feel free to explore these methods now, and then in the future use these methods as necessary for getting help with PowerPoint. For example, you might want to run the Quick Preview option of the Help menu to get a better idea of what you can do in PowerPoint.

Exiting PowerPoint

Patricia has now finished looking at her presentation and is ready to exit PowerPoint. Let's exit PowerPoint.

To exit PowerPoint.

❶ Click **File** on the menu bar, then click **Exit**.

You could also double-click the **Control menu box** on the application window. PowerPoint may display a dialog box with the message "Save changes to **s1file1.ppt**." This message indicates that you have modified the document since last saving it and that you probably need to save it again before exiting.

❷ If the "Save changes" message appeared, click the **Yes button** to save the current version and to exit PowerPoint.

You have now exited PowerPoint. The Program Manager should now be visible on the screen.

Questions

1. In three or four sentences, describe the purpose of the PowerPoint program and what you can do with it.
2. How do you launch PowerPoint from the Windows Program Manager?
3. Explain the function of the following items in the PowerPoint window:
   a. the status bar
   b. the Standard toolbar
   c. the Formatting toolbar
   d. ToolTips
   e. the View toolbar
   f. the Next Slide button
   g. the Drawing toolbar
4. How would you find out information about creating charts (graphs) in PowerPoint?
5. What is the easiest way to get information on an item that appears in the PowerPoint window?
6. How would you do the following:
   a. Scroll to a previous slide?
   b. Change the presentation view?
   c. Save the presentation with a new filename?
7. Define the following PowerPoint terms:
   a. presentation
   b. slide
   c. master
   d. template
   e. outline view
8. What are the four components of a PowerPoint presentation?
9. Name and describe the six questions you should ask yourself when planning a presentation.

E 10. Using the Help feature in PowerPoint, define or describe the following:
   a. the Pick a Look Wizard
   b. the Format Painter
   c. transitions

Tutorial Assignments

In the following Tutorial Assignments, make sure you click the Open an Existing File button (or the Open button on the Standard toolbar) when you launch PowerPoint and then open each file.

Open the file T1FILE1.PPT and immediately save it as S1FILE2.PPT, then do the following:

1. Use the View toolbar to switch to Slide Sorter view to preview all the slides on one screen. How many slides are in the presentation?
2. Use the Slide Sorter view to change slide 3 to slide 2.
3. View the slide show. What is the title of the presentation?
4. Switch from Slide Sorter View to Note Pages View.
5. Zoom the notes page to 100%, then view the notes for all the slides. Which slide has speaker's notes that explain what the Basic Care option emphasizes?
6. Drag the elevator to move to slide 7. What is the purpose of this slide?
7. Use the Next Slide button to go to slide 8. Which month is open enrollment for the health care options?
8. **E** Delete slide 6. *Hint*: Use the Help feature to find out how to delete a slide.
9. Save the presentation using the current filename S1FILE2.PPT.
10. Print slide 1 only. *Note*: In the Print dialog box, select Slide (without Builds) and, if you don't have a color printer, select Black & White.
11. Print the Notes Page for slide 2 only. In the Print dialog box, select Black & White if you don't have a color printer.
12. **E** Using Help, search for help on "build slide." Describe what a build slide is. Which slides in this presentation are build slides?
13. **E** Search for help on "transitions." Describe what a transition is. Which slides in this presentation have a transition? List the steps required to create a transition in a slide.
14. **E** Using the Help Index, look up ClipArt Gallery. In your own words, what is the ClipArt Gallery? Which slides in this presentation include a clip art image?
15. **E** Run the Quick Preview from the Help menu. As you go through the Quick Preview, answer these questions:
    a. List the three types of presentations you can create using PowerPoint.
    b. What features of PowerPoint can you use to organize your thoughts and quickly get you started in making a presentation?
    c. How many AutoLayouts does PowerPoint provide?
    d. List the five items that you can add easily to give your slide "impact."
16. **E** From the Help menu, click the Tip of the Day. What does it say?
17. Close the presentation file.

Case Problem

RSVP Consultants, Inc.

Meryl and Albert Szajnberg own RSVP Consultants, Inc., a wedding and special events consulting company. RSVP's goals include building a new reception center, training five new consultants, and winning the bid to host a local Chamber of Commerce summer celebration.

1. What would be the purpose behind an RSVP presentation to each of the following audiences? In your answer, mention the kind of information each audience would need to know.
    a. investors
    b. RSVP's new employees
    c. potential clients

E 2. Select the type of presentation (recommending a strategy, selling a service or product, providing training, and so forth) RSVP would create for each audience listed in question 1. *Hint*: Run the Quick Preview from the Help menu, then look at the items in the AutoContent Wizard.

3. Identify a likely location (boardroom, auditorium, classroom, or other location) for each of the above three presentations.

4. Select a format (overhead, paper, 35mm slides, or on-screen) for each presentation.

Open the file P1RSVP.PPT and immediately save it as S1RSVP.PPT, then do the following:

5. Switch to Slide Sorter view to preview all the slides. How many slides are in the presentation?

6. Move slide 6 to slide 5 in Slide Sorter view.

7. View the slide show from beginning to end.

8. Indicate which slides would be appropriate for training new employees.

9. Indicate which slides would be appropriate for selling RSVP's services to a prospective client.

E 10. Describe how to hide a slide within a presentation. (*Hint*: Use the "Search for Help on" feature to learn about hidden slides.) How would this feature be helpful in using the current presentation for clients only?

11. Switch to Note Pages view and read the speaker's notes for all the slides. Which slide notes have the word "client" or "clients"?

12. Print the Notes Page for slide 9. *Note*: In the Print dialog box, select Black & White if you don't have a color printer.

13. Save the presentation using the current filename S1RSVP.PPT.

14. Print slide 7 only. *Note*: In the Print dialog box, select Slide (without Builds) and if you don't have a color printer, select Black & White.

E 15. What is WordArt? When would you use it? *Hint*: Use the Help Index to look up this topic.

16. Close the presentation.

T U T O R I A L 2

Creating a Text Slide Show

OBJECTIVES

In this tutorial you will:

- Use the AutoContent Wizard to create an outline
- Edit a presentation in Outline view and Slide view
- Promote and demote items in an outline
- Insert and delete slides
- Use cut-and-paste and drag-and-drop operations
- Change the font, font size, style, and color of text

CASE

Market Research Following Patricia Cuevas's successful presentation to potential investors, Inca Imports International received a collateral commitment from Commercial Financial Bank of Southern California. The commitment secured debt financing for up to $1.5 million to begin construction of a distribution facility in Quito, Ecuador, and to launch a marketing campaign to allow Inca Imports to position itself for further expansion.

Patricia assigned Carl Vetterli, vice president of sales and marketing, the task of identifying potential customers and developing methods to reach them. Carl has scheduled a meeting with Patricia, Angelena Cristenas (vice president of operations), Enrique Hoffmann (director of marketing), and others at which he will review the results of his market research. His presentation will include a demographic profile of Inca Imports' current customers and the results from a customer satisfaction survey, a vision statement of the company's future growth, a list of options for attracting new clients, and recommendations for a marketing strategy.

In this tutorial, you will help Carl create some of the slides for his presentation.

Planning the Presentation

Before starting PowerPoint, Carl identifies the purpose of and audience for his presentation.

- **Purpose for the presentation**: To identify potential customers and ways to reach them
- **Type of presentation**: Recommend a strategy for completing the new marketing campaign
- **Audience for the presentation**: Pat, Angelena, Enrique, and other key staff members in a weekly executive meeting
- **Audience needs**: To understand who our current clients are, and to determine the best way to reach similar new clients
- **Location of the presentation**: Small boardroom
- **Format**: Oral presentation; electronic slide show of five to seven slides

Having planned his presentation, Carl uses PowerPoint to create it.

Using the AutoContent Wizard to Create an Outline

PowerPoint helps you create effective presentations by means of **wizards**, a series of questions that make it easy to establish an organizational structure and consistent style in a presentation. Using the **Pick a Look Wizard**, you can choose a style or design for the slides. Using the **AutoContent Wizard**, you can choose a presentation category such as "Selling a Product, Service, or an Idea," "Recommending a Strategy," or "General." After you have selected the type of presentation you want, the AutoContent Wizard creates a general outline for you to follow.

If you open a new presentation without using the AutoContent Wizard, you must create your own outline one new slide at a time. You will learn how to do this in the section later in this chapter titled "Adding a New Slide and Choosing a Layout." For now, however, you will adapt an outline that PowerPoint automatically creates for you.

Carl decides to use the AutoContent Wizard to quickly create his slides. The AutoContent Wizard will allow Carl to create a title slide and to select a standard outline to guide him in creating his presentation. Let's launch PowerPoint and help Carl use the AutoContent Wizard.

To use the AutoContent Wizard:

1. If necessary, launch PowerPoint.
2. When the startup dialog box appears, click the **AutoContent Wizard button** in the PowerPoint startup dialog box. See Figure 2-1.

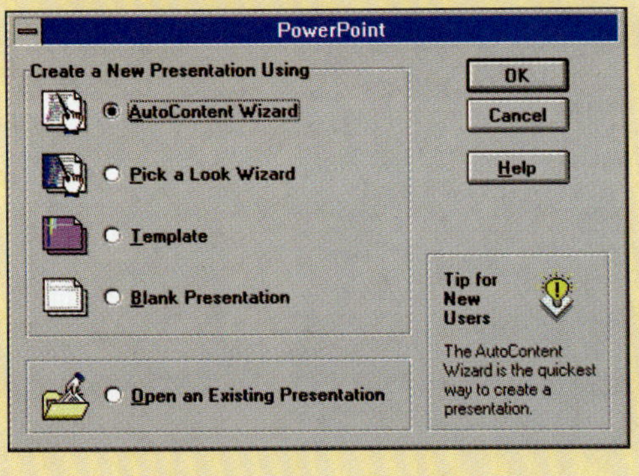

Figure 2-1
PowerPoint startup dialog box

TROUBLE? If the PowerPoint startup dialog box does not appear on your screen, click the New button on the Standard toolbar. When the New Presentation dialog box appears on the screen, click the AutoContent Wizard button.

3. Click the **OK button** or press **[Enter]**.

   PowerPoint displays the first of four AutoContent Wizard dialog boxes. The first dialog box provides information about the function of the AutoContent Wizard.

4. Read the information in the AutoContent Wizard dialog box, then click the **Next button** at the bottom of the dialog box. Step 2 of the AutoContent Wizard appears on the screen. This dialog box creates a title slide for your presentation. The blinking **insertion point** in the text box labeled "What are you going to talk about?" indicates that text will appear at this point when you start typing.

5. Type **Reaching Potential Customers** then press **[Tab]**. The text you typed appears in the first text box, and the text in the second text box, labeled "What is your name?", is highlighted.

6. Type **Carl Vetterli**, press **[Tab]** to move the insertion point to the next text box, labeled "Other information you'd like to include?", and type **Inca Imports International**. Compare your screen to Figure 2-2.

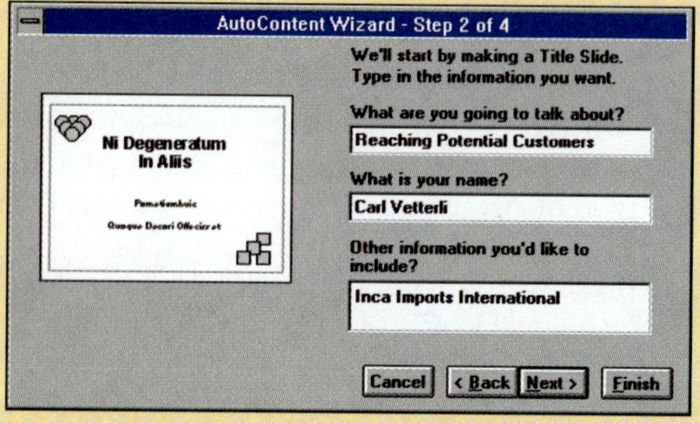

Figure 2-2 AutoContent Wizard, Step 2

TROUBLE? If you accidentally pressed [Enter] before entering all the data, click the Back button in the Step 3 dialog box to return to the Step 2 dialog box, click the mouse pointer in the empty text box, and continue entering the above information.

7. Click the **Next button** to move to Step 3 of the AutoContent Wizard. This dialog box provides six standard formats or outlines for a presentation. Carl wants to recommend a marketing strategy for reaching potential customers.

8. Click the **Recommending a Strategy button**.

   Notice that the list of topics on the left changes to a general outline of presentation ideas for recommending a strategy. See Figure 2-3.

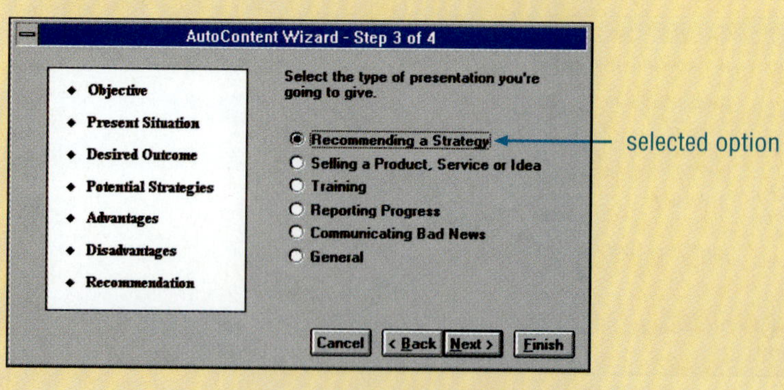

Figure 2-3 AutoContent Wizard, Step 3

❾ Click the **Next button**, read the information in the Step 4 dialog box, and then click the **Finish button**.

The Outline view appears, with a standard outline of a presentation for recommending a strategy already filled in. A Cue Cards screen with "Tips for Working in PowerPoint" may appear on the right. See Figure 2-4.

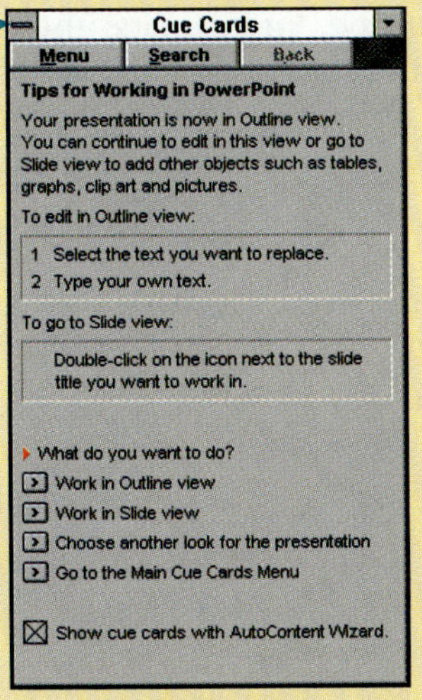

Figure 2-4
Cue Cards window

❿ If the Cue Cards screen appears, read the information, then remove the screen by double-clicking the **Control menu box** of the Cue Cards window. Your screen should look like Figure 2-5. (If necessary, click the **Maximize button** in the presentation window.)

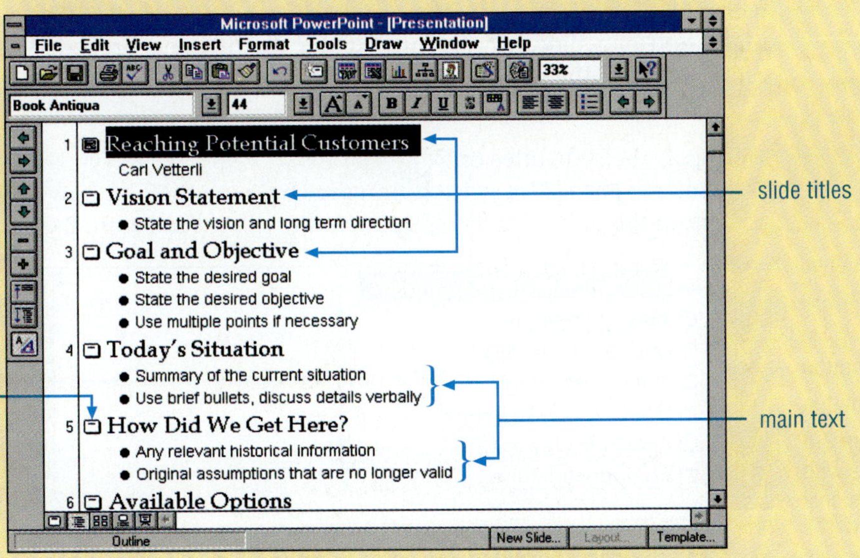

Figure 2-5
Presentation window in Outline view

TROUBLE? If you accidentally click the main Control menu box of PowerPoint, you'll get the message, "Save changes to Presentations?" If this happens, click the Cancel button to cancel the exit from PowerPoint, and then double-click the Control menu box of the Cue Cards window.

Adapting an AutoContent Outline

After completing the AutoContent Wizard, PowerPoint displays an outline consisting of Carl's title slide (Slide 1) and additional slides with text, called placeholders, suggesting ideas for the presentation. A **placeholder** is a region of a window reserved for inserting text or graphics. To adapt the AutoContent outline to your own presentation, you **select**, or highlight, the placeholders, one at a time, and replace them with your own text. Because Outline view allows you to see the text of your presentation as a whole rather than as individual slides, Outline view is usually the easiest view for working with text. You can also apply formatting changes to the text and change the order of the slides in Outline view.

DESIGN PRINCIPLE WINDOW

Principles for Creating Effective Text Presentations

- Think of your presentation as a visual map to your oral presentation.
- Show your organization by using overviews, by making headings larger than subheadings, and by numbering steps to show sequence.
- Follow the **6x6 rule**: Use six or fewer items per screen, and use incomplete sentences of six or fewer words. Omit unnecessary articles, pronouns, and adjectives.
- Keep phrases parallel.
- Make sure your text is appropriate for your purpose and audience.

Each main heading of the outline, called the **title** of a slide, appears at the left, along with a slide icon and slide number, as shown in Figure 2-5. The subheadings, called the **main text** of a slide, are indented under the title and preceded by a bullet. PowerPoint can display just the titles of the slides or the entire outline with titles and main text.

To display the slide titles only:

1. Click the **Show Titles button** on the Outlining toolbar. PowerPoint hides the main text of the outline and displays only the titles. See Figure 2-6.

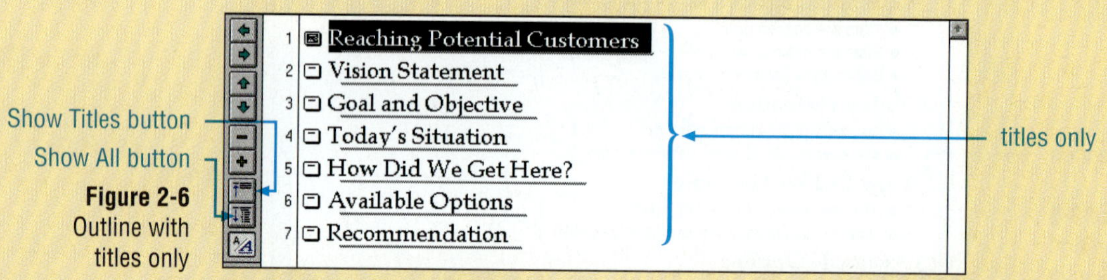

Figure 2-6 Outline with titles only

2. Click the **Show All button** on the Outlining toolbar to display both the titles and main text of the outline.

Carl wants to add his own text to the Vision Statement, which is slide 2. Let's replace the main text in this slide now.

To replace the main text in a slide:

❶ Make sure the presentation window is maximized, if necessary, by clicking the **Maximize button** in the upper-right corner of the presentation window. (Your presentation window may already be maximized.) If necessary, drag the horizontal scroll button to the far left so you can see the left edge of the outline text.

❷ Position the mouse pointer before the "S" in the sentence "State the vision and long term direction," which is located beneath the title of slide 2. The pointer changes to I.

❸ Press and hold the mouse button, drag the pointer to the end of the line, then release the mouse button. Your screen should look similar to Figure 2-7. This method of selecting text is called **dragging**. To replace the selected text, just start typing.

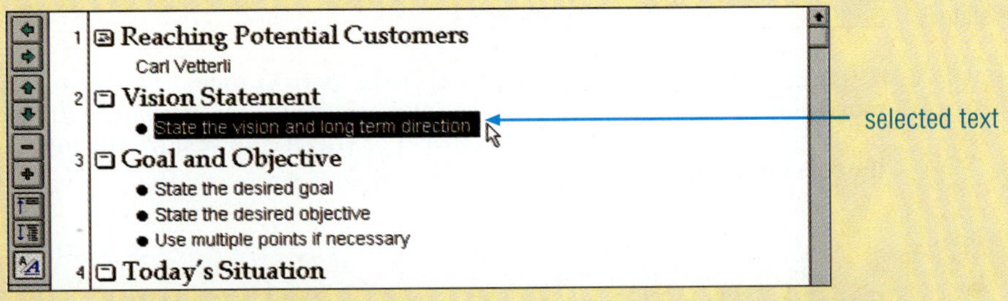

Figure 2-7
Text selected for replacement

❹ Type **Inca can improve the quality of its produce**. Your screen should now look like Figure 2-8.

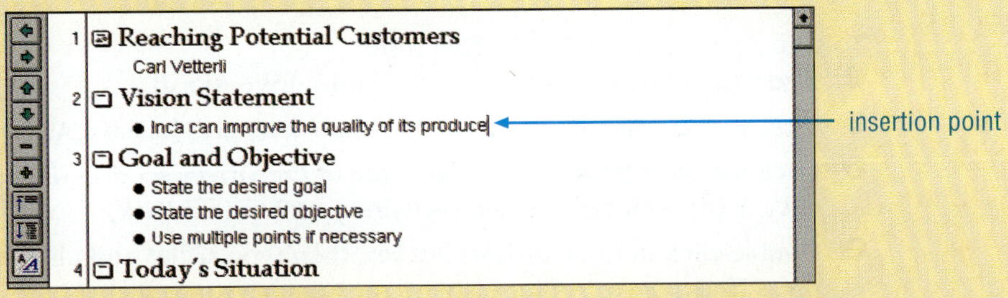

Figure 2-8
New text in slide 2

Notice that as soon as you started typing, the selected text disappeared as the new phrase you typed appeared.

Carl has two more bullets he wants to add to the Vision Statement slide. Let's do that now.

To add new text to the outline:

❶ Press **[Enter]**. When you press [Enter], PowerPoint automatically inserts a bullet for the next item in the list, and the insertion point appears to the right of the bullet.

❷ Type **Inca can sell more produce to more customers** and press **[Enter]**.

❸ Type **Inca can become the clear market leader in Southern California** and press **[Enter]**. Your screen should now look like Figure 2-9.

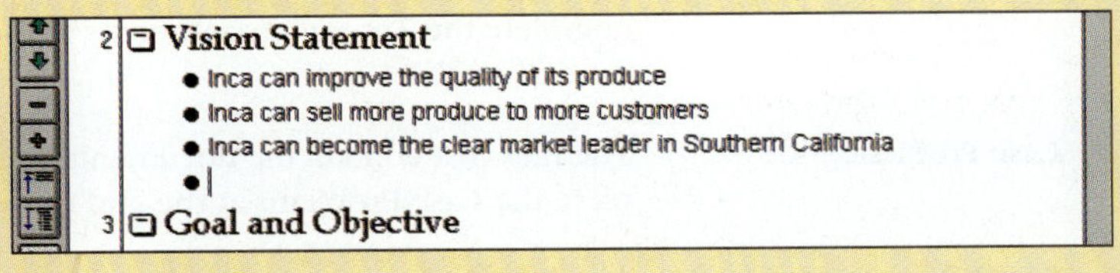

Figure 2-9
Completed bulleted items in slide 2

Carl realizes that he really wants only three items in the list, not four. He deletes the fourth bullet.

❹ Press **[Backspace]** to delete the fourth bullet and move the insertion point to the end of the preceding line.

Next Carl wants to replace the placeholder text in slide 3, "Goal and Objective."

❺ Make the changes in slide 3 using the text in Figure 2-10.

Figure 2-10
Complete text of slide 3

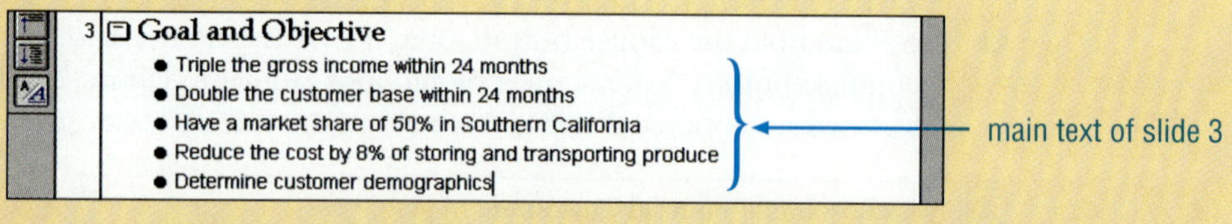

TROUBLE? If you make typographical errors, correct them. Use the normal insertion-point movement keys ([→], [←], [↑], [↓]) to move the insertion point to the location of the mistake or click I at the location; use [Backspace] or [Delete] to remove the mistake, and then retype the text correctly.

Saving the Presentation for the First Time

Carl has made substantial progress on his presentation and he decides to save the changes.

To save a presentation for the first time:

❶ Insert the PowerPoint Student Disk into drive A or B.

❷ Click the **Save button** on the Standard toolbar. The Save As dialog box appears.

❸ Click the **Down arrow** on the right side of the Drives section of the dialog box, then click **a:** (or whichever drive contains your Student Disk).

❹ Double-click in the **File Name text box**, then type **s2file1** and click the **OK button** or press **[Enter]**. PowerPoint displays the Summary Info dialog box.

❺ Click the **OK button** to close the Summary Info dialog box.

PowerPoint saves the file to the disk using the filename S2FILE1.PPT. That name now appears in the Slide window title bar.

In this book, the four tutorials on PowerPoint involve many files. Therefore, we use filenames that will help you and your instructor recognize the origin and content of the various documents. To name these files so you can recognize their contents, we have categorized them as follows:

File Category	Description
Tutorial Cases	The files you use to work through each tutorial
Tutorial Assignments	The files that contain the documents you need to complete the Tutorial Assignments at the end of each tutorial
Case Problems	The files that contain the documents you need to complete the Case Problems at the end of each tutorial
Saved Document	Any document you have saved

Let's take the filename S1FILE1.PPT, for example. At first glance this filename might appear to have no meaning, but it does contain meaningful abbreviations. The first character of the filename identifies the file as one of the four categories given above, as shown here:

If the first character is:	The file category is:
C	Tutorial **C**ase
T	**T**utorial Assignment
P	Case **P**roblem
S	**S**aved Document

Thus, S1FILE1.PPT is a document that you have saved.

The second character of the document filename identifies the tutorial from which the file comes. Thus, S1FILE1.PPT is a file you saved from Tutorial 1. The remaining six characters of the filename identify the specific file. All documents in the tutorials are named FILE, followed by a number. Each time you save a file, you will increase the number after FILE by 1.

If you want to take a break and resume the tutorial at a later time, you can do so now. If you exit PowerPoint, launch the program again when you want to resume working, open the presentation file S2FILE1.PPT, and select Outline view. Then continue with this tutorial.

Editing the Presentation in Outline View

As Carl reviews the text of the first three slides, he realizes that in a slide presentation, each text item should be as short as possible. It is easier for the audience to read short phrases. In addition, he knows that he will be conveying most of the information orally, so the main text doesn't have to be complete sentences.

Carl decides to apply the "6 x 6 Rule" as much as possible and simplify the text in slide 2. Because the audience will be aware that Carl is talking about Inca Imports International, the company name is unnecessary. Similarly, articles ("the," "a"), many possessive pronouns ("your," "its"), and most adjectives ("high," "clear," "very") can safely be left out of titles and the main text. Therefore, Carl decides to change "Inca can improve the quality of its produce" to "Improve quality of produce." Carl also realizes that by changing the title of slide 3 from "Goal and Objective," to "Two-Year Goals," he can delete the words "within 24 months" from the bulleted list.

To edit the outline:

❶ Using Figure 2-11 as a guide, change the text of slides 2 and 3 of Carl's presentation by dragging I to select text and then deleting it or retyping it.

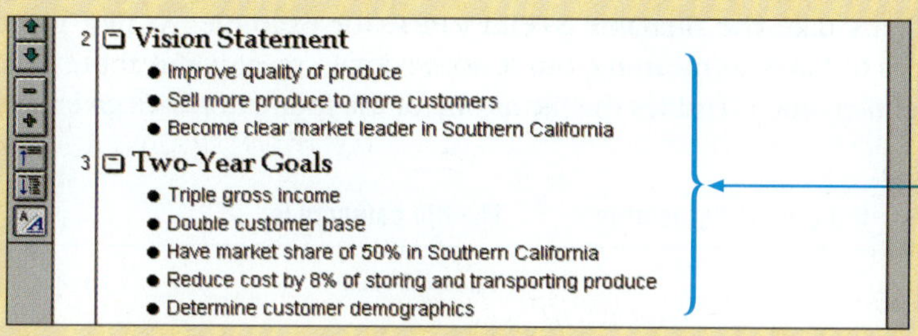

Figure 2-11 Revised text in slides 2 and 3

Moving Text Up and Down in Outline View

As Carl reads through the text of the first three slides, he decides to switch the second and third items under "Two-Year Goals." Let's reverse the order of these items now.

To move an item of text in Outline view:

1. Move the mouse pointer to the left of the text (for example, on the bullet) "Have market share of 50% in Southern California," so that the mouse pointer becomes ✥, and click once.

   PowerPoint highlights the text of that item.

2. Click the **Move Up Arrow button** on the Outlining toolbar.

   PowerPoint moves the highlighted item up one position in the list, so the second and third items are switched. See Figure 2-12.

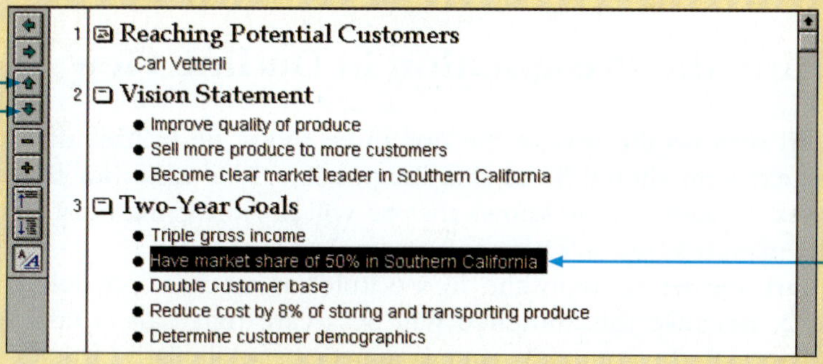

Figure 2-12 Moved bulleted item

You can use this same method to move entire slides. To move a slide, click ✥ on the slide icon of the slide you want to move, then click the Move Up button or the Move Down button on the Outlining toolbar to move the slide.

Promoting and Demoting the Outline Text

While reviewing slide 3, Carl realizes that he needs to present more information on his customer demographic study. Rather than having "Determine customer demographics" as the last item of the main text of slide 3, Carl wants that phrase to be a title of a separate slide. Instead of deleting the bulleted item and then retyping it as a new slide title, Carl will promote the item from main text to slide title. To **promote** an item means to increase the outline level of an item, for example, to change a bulleted item to a slide title. To **demote** an item means to decrease the outline level, for example, to change a slide title to a bulleted item within another slide.

Let's promote the item "Determine customer demographics" in order to create the new slide.

To promote an item:

❶ Click I anywhere within the bulleted item "Determine customer demographics" in slide 3.

❷ Click the **Promote (Indent less) button**. This button is located in two places: on the Outlining toolbar and on the Formatting toolbar.

When you click the Promote button, the text moves left and increases in size, and the new slide icon appears to the left of the text. The new slide becomes slide 4, and "Today's Situation" becomes slide 5, as shown in Figure 2-13. Because the title of slide 4 is wordy, Carl decides to edit it.

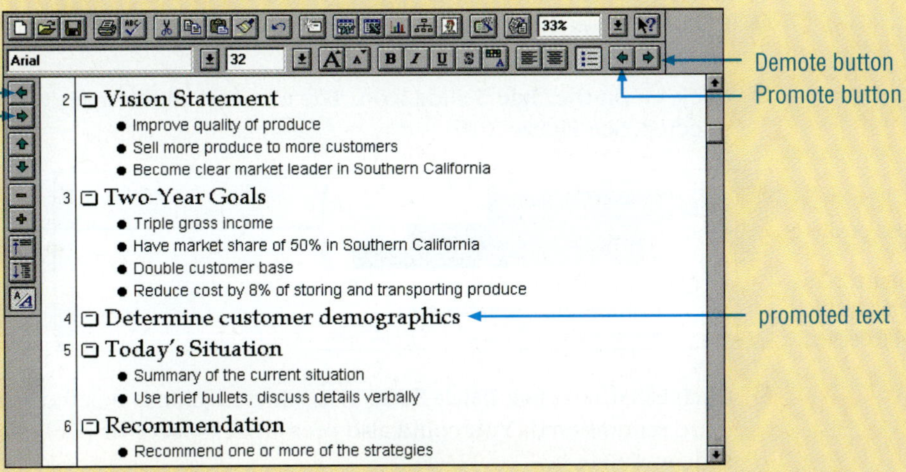

Figure 2-13
Promoted text (new slide)

❸ Change the title "**Determine customer demographics**" to "**Customer Demographics.**"

Carl is now ready to add the bulleted items beneath the title of slide 4. However, because the current outline level is a slide title, any text Carl adds will be input at the same level, that is, as a slide title. To add main text, therefore, Carl has to move down a level in the outline. He can do this by using the Demote command.

To demote an item:

❶ Click I at the end of the title "Customer Demographics," then press **[Enter]**. PowerPoint creates a new slide 5.

❷ Click the **Demote (Indent More) button** on the Outlining or Formatting toolbar to change the outline level from slide title to main text and to indent.

❸ Type the main text of slide 4 as shown in Figure 2-14. Carefully check to make sure you have typed the information correctly. Make any necessary corrections.

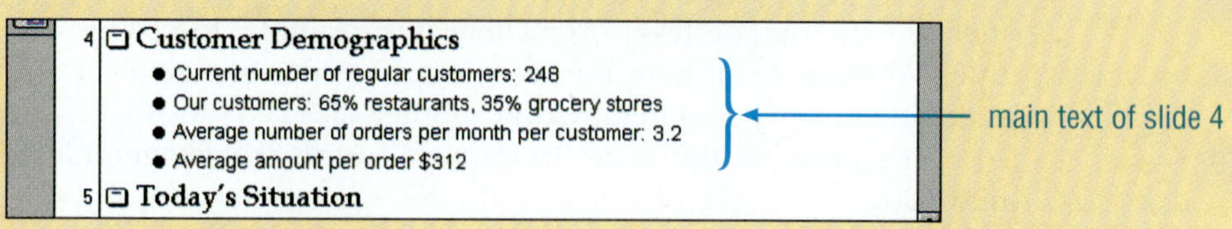

Figure 2-14 Text of slide 4

Deleting a Slide

Carl feels that in his presentation he doesn't need slides on "Today's Situation," "How Did We Get Here?" or "Available Options," which are three of the default titles in the "Recommending a Strategy" outline. You can delete a slide in any view except Slide Show. Carl decides to delete these three slides now.

To delete a slide:

1. Click the **Down Scroll arrow** on the vertical scroll bar until you can see all of slide 5 on the screen.
2. Click ✥ on the slide 5 slide icon. The title and all the main text of slide 5 is selected. See Figure 2-15.

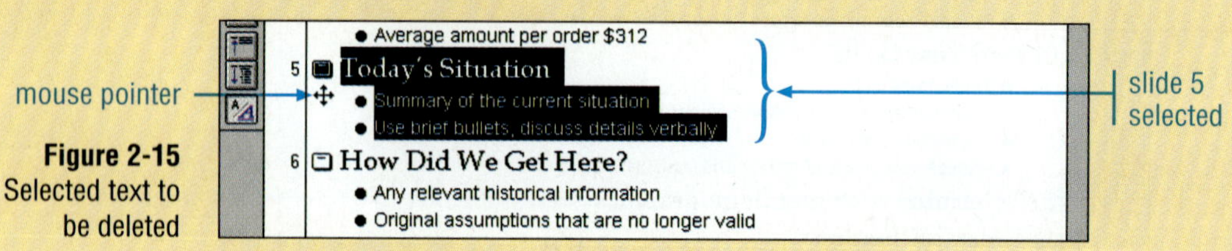

Figure 2-15 Selected text to be deleted

3. Click **Edit**, then click **Delete Slide**. The selected slide is deleted and all the slides after it are renumbered. You could also press [Backspace] or [Del] after selecting the slide to delete it.
4. Repeat steps 1 and 2 for the slides with the titles "How Did We Get Here?" and "Available Options" to delete them.

The last title in Carl's presentation is "Recommendations." Let's create that slide now.

To create the last slide:

1. Edit the title of slide 5 to change "**Recommendation**" to "**Recommendations.**"
2. Edit the main text of slide 5 so that the bulleted items match those in Figure 2-16.

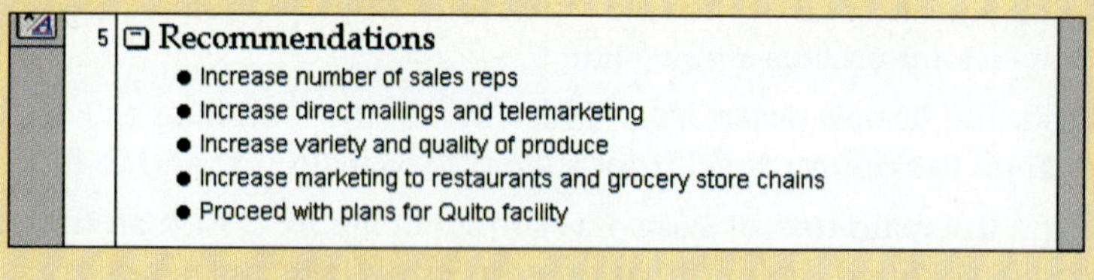

Figure 2-16 Text of slide 5

Carl has adapted and edited his presentation in Outline view and has completed the five slides of his presentation. He decides to use Slide view to see how his presentation looks.

Viewing Slides in Slide View

Viewing your presentation in Outline view doesn't show you how each of your slides will look when you actually make your presentation. To see the slides, you need to change to Slide view. Let's view the first three slides in Slide view.

To show slides in Slide view:

1. Scroll the presentation window so you can see the beginning of the outline, then click the mouse pointer anywhere within the text of slide 1. This makes slide 1 the current slide, so that when you switch to Slide view, slide 1 will appear on the screen.
2. Click the **Slide View button** on the View toolbar.

   You could also click **View**, then click **Slides**. PowerPoint displays slide 1 in the presentation window. After looking over the slide, view the next slide.
3. Click the **Next Slide button** at the bottom of the vertical scroll bar. PowerPoint displays slide 2, "Vision Statement."

   TROUBLE? If PowerPoint doesn't advance to the next slide, you may have clicked the Previous Slide button. Try step 3 again, this time clicking the Next Slide button. If you're not sure which is the Next Slide button, move the mouse pointer to one of the buttons in the lower-right corner of the presentation window and read the ToolTip.

   After looking at slide 2, view slide 3.
4. Drag the **elevator** down until the slide identifier shows that you are on slide 3, as shown in Figure 2-17, then release the mouse button.

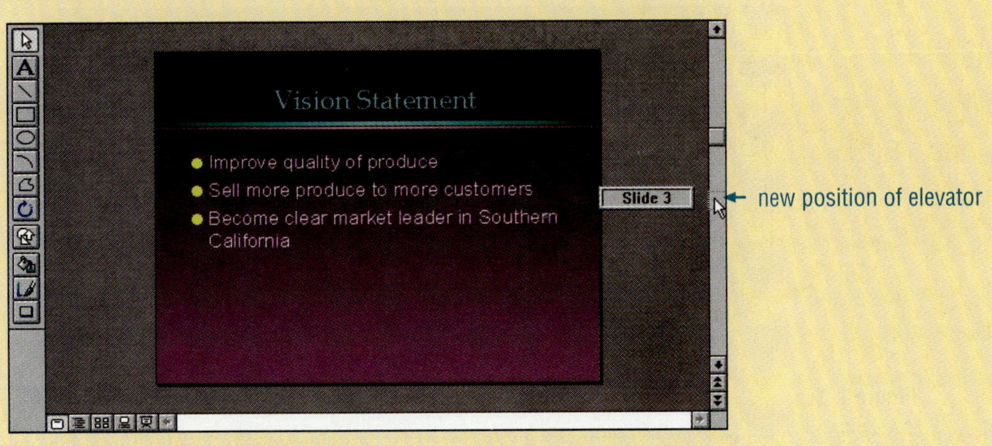

Figure 2-17
Moving elevator to slide 3

As you can see, Slide view allows you to see exactly how the slides will appear during Carl's presentation.

Moving Text Using Cut and Paste

Cut and paste is an important way to move text in PowerPoint. To **cut** means to remove text (or some other item) from the document and place it on the Windows clipboard. The **clipboard** is an area where text and graphics that have been cut or copied are stored until you act on them further. To **paste** means to transfer a copy of the text from the clipboard into the document. To perform a cut-and-paste operation, you simply highlight the text you want to move, cut it, and then paste the text where you want it.

As Carl looks at slide 3, "Two-Year Goals," of his PowerPoint presentation, he decides the fourth bullet sounds a little awkward. He wants to move the phrase "by 8%" to the end of the fourth item, so that it becomes "Reduce cost of storing and transporting produce by 8%."

REFERENCE WINDOW

Cutting and Pasting (Moving) Text

- Select the text you want to move.
- Cut the selected text by clicking the Cut button on the Standard toolbar.
- Move the insertion point to the target location in the presentation.
- Paste the text back into the presentation by clicking the Paste button on the Standard toolbar.

Let's change the text using the cut-and-paste method.

To move text using cut and paste:

❶ Make sure slide 3 appears in the PowerPoint window in Slide view, as shown in Figure 2-18.

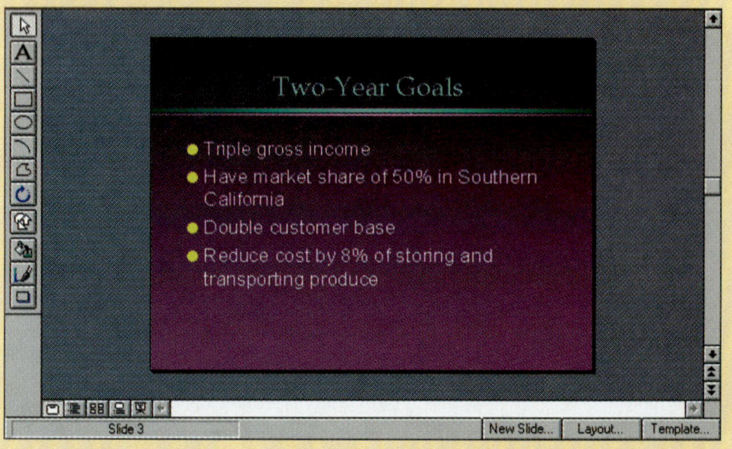

Figure 2-18
Slide 3

❷ Click I anywhere on the main text of the slide. A selection box appears around the bulleted items to indicate that the text is selected, and the text is highlighted in color.

❸ Select the phrase "by 8%" in the fourth item of slide 3 by dragging the mouse pointer over it. See Figure 2-19.

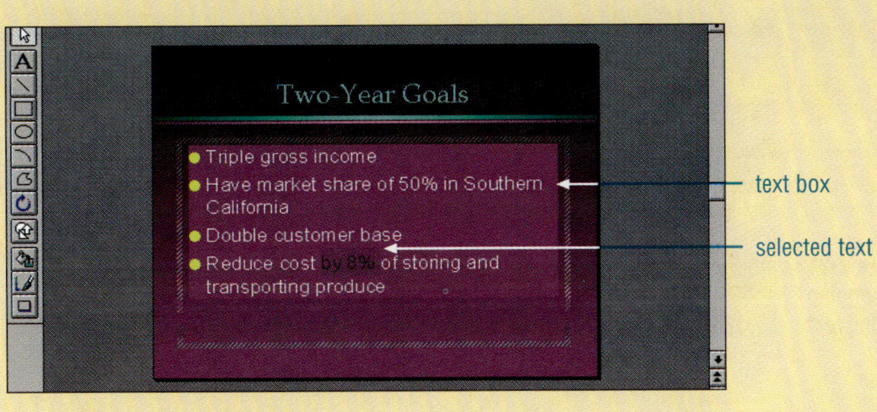

Figure 2-19
Selected text for cut and paste

❹ Click the **Cut button** on the Standard toolbar. The phrase disappears from the screen and is pasted onto the clipboard.

❺ Click I at the end of the phrase, "Reduce cost of storing and transporting produce." This puts the insertion point at the location where you want to paste the text back into the slide.

TROUBLE? The insertion point may be hard to see with the PowerPoint default color scheme. If you can't see the insertion point, don't worry about it. Make sure you clicked I in the correct place, then go on to the next step.

❻ Click the **Paste button** on the Standard toolbar. The phrase "by 8%" appears again in the slide, but this time at the end of the item. See Figure 2-20.

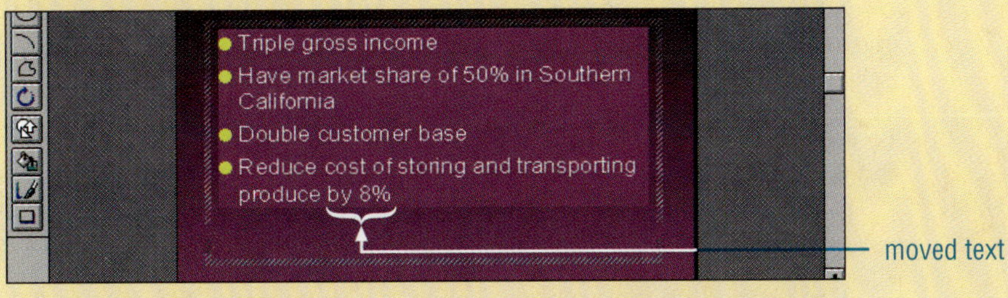

Figure 2-20
Slide after pasting text

To copy selected text rather than move it, click the Copy button on the Standard toolbar instead of the Cut button.

Moving Text Using Drag and Drop

In addition to cut and paste, you can use **drag and drop** to move text in PowerPoint. You simply select the text by dragging the mouse pointer over it, press and hold down the left mouse button while you drag the text, and then release the mouse button.

Carl wants to move the words "of 50%" from the middle to the end of the bulleted item in the main text of slide 3. Let's move the phrase now.

To move text using drag and drop:

❶ Select the phrase "**of 50%.**"

❷ Move the mouse pointer within the region of the selected text, press and hold the mouse button, drag the mouse pointer to the right of the word "California" in the same item of the main text, then release the mouse button.

❸ Click anywhere outside the text area to deselect the text. The phrase "of 50%" moves from the middle of the bulleted item to the end of the item. See Figure 2-21.

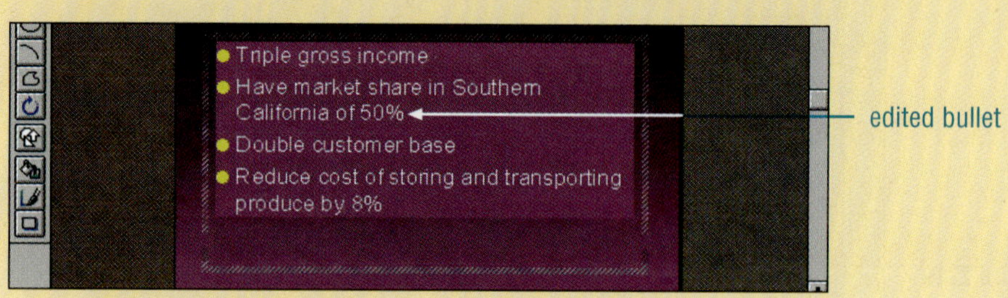

Figure 2-21 Slide after dragging and dropping text

Cut and paste and drag and drop are both effective in moving text from one location to another. You can use both methods in any view except Slide Show.

Adding a New Slide and Choosing a Layout

Carl created his presentation using the AutoContent Wizard, witch gave him a ready-made outline to adapt to his own purpose. However, you don't have to use a wizard to create a presentation. You can create it from scratch using the Blank Presentation button in the PowerPoint startup dialog box. PowerPoint displays blank slides to which you add your own text.

Carl decides his presentation needs a slide that summarizes Inca Import's new marketing plan, so he decides to add a new slide. Let's add the slide in slide view now.

To add a slide in slide view:

❶ With slide 3 still in the presentation window, click the **New Slide button** on the status line. PowerPoint displays the New Slide dialog box. You could also click the **Insert New Slide button** on the Standard toolbar.

The New Slide dialog box appears on the screen. See Figure 2-22.

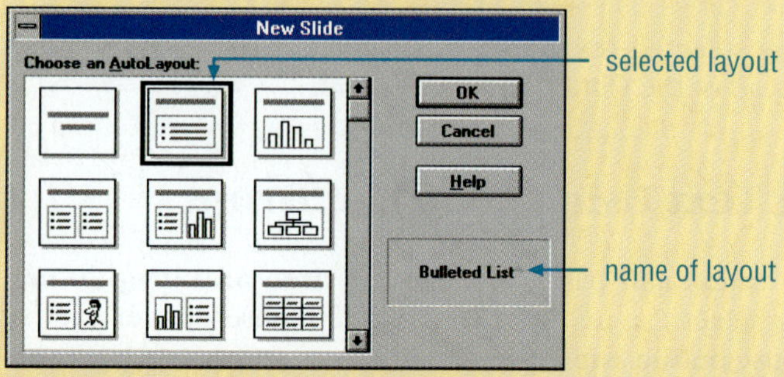

Figure 2-22 New Slide dialog box

When you add a slide, you must decide where you want the placeholders for titles, text, and graphics to go. You do this by choosing an **AutoLayout**, a ready-made format for these placeholders. You can also choose a blank layout.

❷ Drag the **elevator** on the AutoLayout scroll bar to the bottom of the scroll bar.

❸ Click on a few of the AutoLayouts and read the name in the lower-right corner of the dialog box.

4. Click the **Blank slide layout**, which is the last layout in the list. You would click this layout if you wanted to set up your own layout. Carl wants his new slide to be a bulleted list.
5. Drag the **elevator** on the AutoLayout scroll bar to the top of the scroll bar, then click the second layout in the top row, titled "Bulleted List," as shown in Figure 2-22.
6. Click the **OK button**. PowerPoint inserts a new slide containing a title and main text placeholder for the bulleted list.
7. Click the **title placeholder** (where the slide says "Click to add title") and type **Our New Marketing Campaign**.
8. Click the **main text placeholder** and type the three bulleted items shown in Figure 2-23.
9. Click anywhere outside the text areas to deselect the text box. Make sure your slide 4 looks like Figure 2-23.

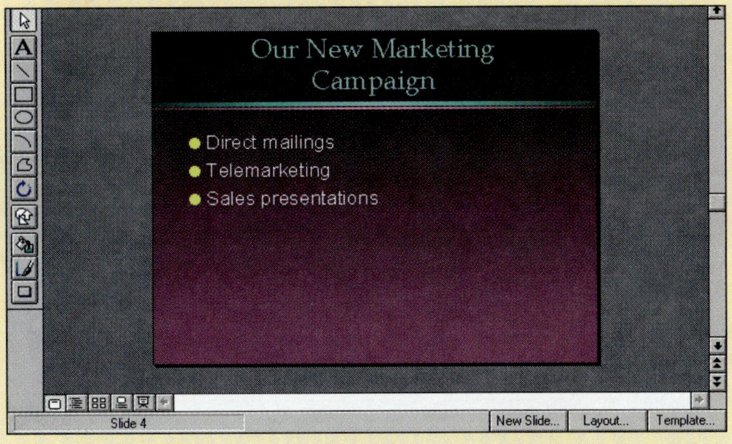

Figure 2-23
Completed new slide 4

Changing the Template

When you use the AutoContent Wizard or open a blank presentation, PowerPoint provides a predetermined **template**, that is, the colors and design on the background of the text, and the type style of the titles, accents, and other text. The default template that PowerPoint uses with the Recommending a Strategy option in the AutoContent Wizard is the double lines (dbllines) template; double lines divide the title from the main text, the background is maroon, the title text is green, and the main text is white. You can change the default template to another one from among more than 100 that PowerPoint provides. To change the template, you either click the Template button in the status bar or you can use the Pick a Look Wizard.

Carl wants to change the template for his presentation. Let's change the template now.

To change the template:

1. Click the **Template button** in the status bar. The Presentation Template dialog box appears. See Figure 2-24.

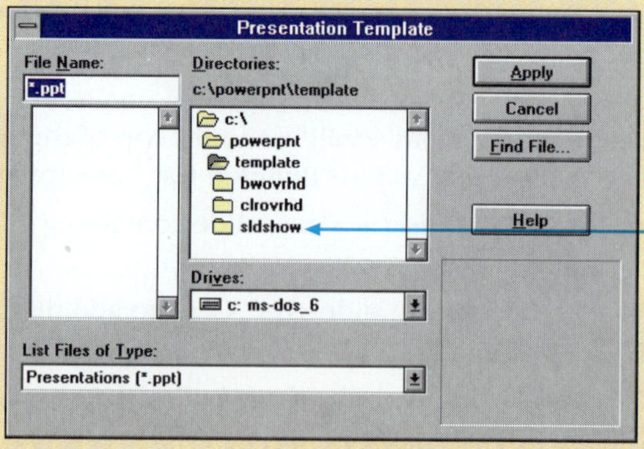

Figure 2-24 Presentation template dialog box

TROUBLE? Your screen may show a list of .ppt template files. If so, skip to step 3.

❷ Double-click the sldshow folder in the Directories section of the dialog box.

❸ Scroll the template names in the File Name list box until you see **sidebars.ppt**, then click that name. The selected template design appears in the preview box at the lower-right of the dialog box.

TROUBLE? If you do not have a template SIDEBARS.PPT installed on your computer, choose any other template you like.

❹ Click the **Apply button** to change the template for all the slides in the presentation. The new template will appear on all the slides in the presentation. Carl wants to see what the new template looks like in the title slide.

❺ Move to slide 1 by dragging the **elevator** to the top of the scroll bar. The title slide appears in the window. See Figure 2-25.

Figure 2-25 Title slide with template

Formatting Text

When Carl created his presentation, he used PowerPoint's default fonts for his slide show. A **font** is a set of characters (letters, digits, and other characters such as !, @, and *) that have a certain design and appearance. Each font has a name, such as Courier, Times Roman, or Univers (Figure 2-26). The current font is listed on the left of the Formatting toolbar. The default font in the SIDEBARS.PPT template is Times New Roman. (Your toolbar might indicate a different font, depending on your printer and on which fonts are installed on your system.) The height of a font is measured in points. A **point** is 1/72 of an inch.

Courier
Times Roman
Univers

Figure 2-26
Example fonts

You can change the font, the font size, the font style (bold, italic, underlined), and the font color. PowerPoint does a good job selecting fonts for the slides; however, there may be times when you want to change the defaults chosen by PowerPoint.

DESIGN PRINCIPLE WINDOW

Typography Guidelines

- The size of the text should reflect the importance level of the text, that is, titles should be larger than main text.
- Use large fonts (24 through 60 points).
- Vary type styles to provide emphasize, but remember that having too much emphasis is the same as having none.
- Words in all uppercase can decrease reading speed. It's easier to read words in mostly lowercase letters because the shapes of the letters help the reader see the words as a unit.
- Bold, italic, and underlining are difficult to distinguish on-screen.

REFERENCE WINDOW

Changing the Font, Font Size, and Font Style

- Select the text that you want to change.
- Click the appropriate button on the Formatting toolbar.

To change the Font, click the Font down arrow and choose the desired font. To change the Font size, click the Font Size down arrow and choose the desired size, or click the Increase/Decrease Font Size buttons. To change the Font style, click the Bold, Italics, Underline, or Text Shadow buttons.

Carl now decides that his name and the company name on the title should be in two different colors rather than the same color text.

DESIGN PRINCIPLE WINDOW

Principles of Using Color on a Slide

- Color can focus the reader's attention.
- Color can establish understanding through associations (for example, red as a warning).
- Color can reveal organization and pattern by using similar colors for related ideas.
- Too much color can be distracting and slow down reading and comprehension.

Carl decides to change the color of the text "Inca Imports International" in slide 1. PowerPoint doesn't allow you to change the color of the text from Outline view, but you can change the color from Slide view.

REFERENCE WINDOW

Changing the Color of the Text

- Make sure you are in Slide view.
- Select the text that you want to change.
- Click the Text Color button on the Formatting toolbar.
- Choose the desired font color.

Let's change the color of the company name.

To change the color of the text:

1. Click anywhere on the company name, then drag I to select the phrase "Inca Imports International."
2. Click the **Text Color button** on the Formatting toolbar. PowerPoint displays a small grid of colors.
3. Click the **yellow tile** (small square) on the Text Color menu. PowerPoint changes the color of the company name to yellow, although you can't see that color yet because the text is selected.
4. Deselect the text by clicking the mouse pointer anywhere in the slide except on text. The title slide now looks like Figure 2-27.

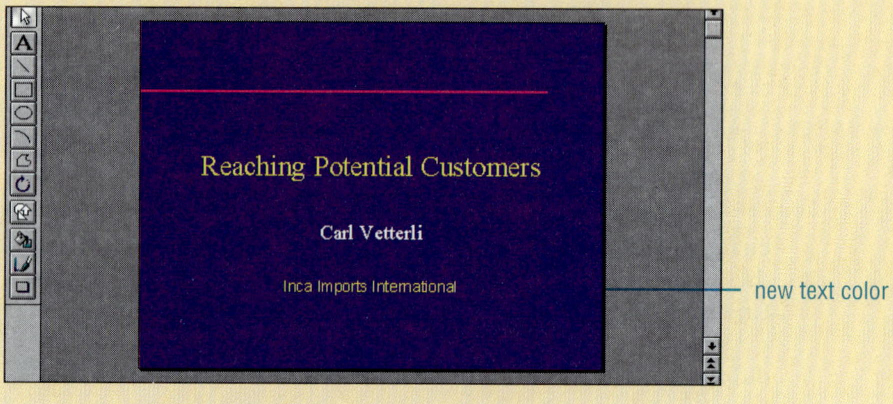

Figure 2-27 Slide 1 after changing text color

By making appropriate changes in the font style and color, you can improve the appearance and readability of the text within your slide show.

Saving the Final Version of the Presentation

Having completed the presentation, Carl is now ready to save the final version. Because he has saved the presentation previously, he can simple click the Save button to save the current version of the file over the now obsolete version.

To save a file that has been saved previously:

1. Make sure your Student Disk is in the disk drive.
2. Click the **Save button** on the Standard toolbar. PowerPoint saves the file using its current filename, S2FILE1.PPT.

A copy of the updated presentation is now on your Student Disk.

Viewing the Completed Slide Show

Carl wants to see his completed slide show.

To view the completed presentation as a slide show:

1. Make sure you're viewing slide 1 in Slide view. If you were in Outline view, the insertion point would need to be somewhere within the text of slide 1. This ensures that when you begin the Slide Show, slide 1 appears on the screen first.
2. Click the **Slide Show button** on the View toolbar.
3. After you read a slide, click the **left mouse button** or press **[Spacebar]** to advance to the next slide. Continue advancing until you've see the entire slide show and PowerPoint returns to Slide view or Outline view.

Printing the Presentation

Carl decides he will print his presentation as handouts in order to have a hard copy for his records. Let's do that now.

To print handouts of the presentation:

1. From Slide view or Outline view, click **File**, then click **Print**. PowerPoint displays the Print dialog box. Don't click the Print button on the Standard toolbar or PowerPoint will immediately start printing without letting you change the print settings.
2. Click the **Down arrow** next to the Print What box, and select **Handouts (2 slides per page)**.
3. If you're using a blank-and-white printer, click the **Black & White** checkbox on the Print dialog box. See Figure 2-28.

choose Handouts

select Black & White

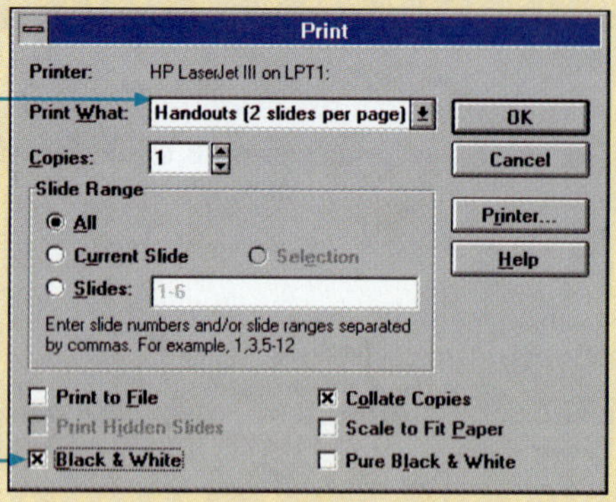

Figure 2-28
Print dialog box

❹ Click the **OK button** to print the slides.

Be patient. Graphics usually take a long time to print, even on a relatively fast laser printer.

❺ To see how the slides look as a group, click the **Slide Sorter View icon** . You should have three handouts, each containing two slides. Compare your handouts with the six slides shown in Figure 2-29.

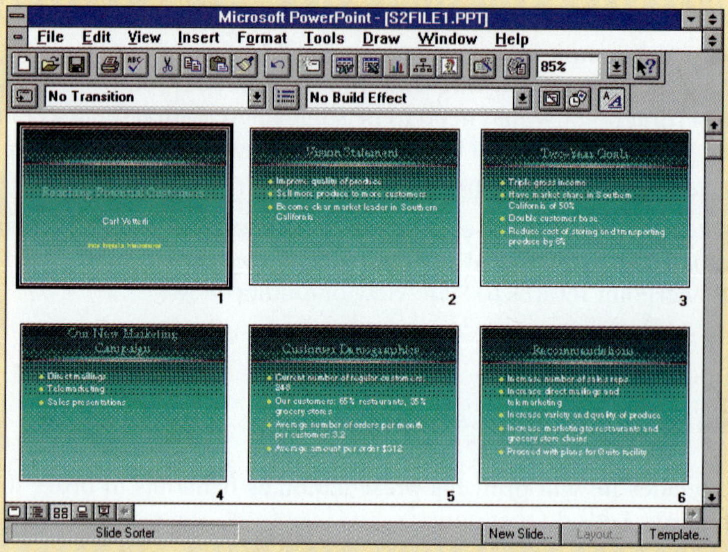

Figure 2-29
Completed presentation in Slide Sorter view

Carl now has a hard copy of his presentation.

Having created, edited, saved, and printed his presentation, Carl is now ready to exit PowerPoint.

To exit PowerPoint:

❶ Click **File**, then click **Exit** (or double-click the **Control menu box** in the upper-left corner of the PowerPoint window).

❷ If PowerPoint asks if you want to save changes to the presentation file, click the **Yes button**.

Your computer screen should now be back to the Program Manager.

■ ■ ■

Questions

1. Describe the purpose of the AutoContent Wizard.
2. Which key(s) do you press or buttons do you click to do the following:
   a. Delete text in Outline view
   b. Move between Outline view and Slide view
   c. Change the color of a font
   d. Increase the size of a font
3. Write a list of steps required to do each of the following:
   a. Promote an item from the main text to a slide title
   b. Change a slide title to a bulleted item within another slide
   c. Delete a slide in Outline view
   d. Add a slide in Outline view
   e. Move text using cut and paste in any view
   f. Move text using drag and drop in any view
   g. Change placeholder text in Outline view
4. Explain the 6 x 6 rule.
5. Explain the meaning of the following terms:
   a. placeholder
   b. title
   c. main text
   d. bullet
   e. promote
   f. demote
   g. font
   h. points
6. Explain the difference between Outline view and Slide view and the benefits of each view.
7. How do you select the text of a placeholder?
8. E After you've made an editing change in PowerPoint, how do you undo it?
9. Give one advantage and one disadvantage of a cut-and-paste operation versus a drag-and-drop operation.
10. Describe how to change the presentation template.

Tutorial Assignments

In the following Tutorial Assignments, make sure you click the Open an Existing File button when you launch PowerPoint (or the Open button on the Standard toolbar) and then open each file. After working with a presentation and saving your changes, close the presentation.

Open the file T2FILE1.PPT, save the file as S2FILE2.PPT and do the following:

1. In Outline view, delete the unnecessary articles "a," "an," and "the" from the main text.
2. In Slide view, change the color of the title of slide 1 from white to red.
3. In Outline view, move the second item in slide 3, "Will develop slide presentation," down so that it becomes the third (last) item in the main text.
4. In slide 4, the third item of the main text is "Step #2. Establishing Contact with Potential Customers." Promote that item to become a slide title (new slide 5).
5. In the current slide 6, demote the second, third, and fourth bulleted items so that they appear indented beneath the first item, "Organize data for our market advantage:".
6. In slides 4 through 7, change the phrases "Step #1," "Step #2," "Step #3," and "Step #4" (but not the text that follows these phrases in the slide titles) to another sans serif font, such as Arial or Futura.
7. Edit the main text of slide 8 so that the phrase "Must hire" becomes simply "Hire."
8. In slide 2, move (through cut and paste or drag and drop) the phrase "by telephone" so it immediately follows the phrase "Follow up" in the same item of the main text.
9. E Move the entire slide 9 ("Key Issues") up to become slide 8, so that "Becoming More Effective" is the last slide. Hint: Drag the slide icon in Outline view from one position to another.
10. E In slide 2, underline the phrase "New Marketing Campaign" by selecting the phrase and then by clicking the Underline button on the Standard toolbar.
11. E Check the spelling within the presentation by using the Spelling button on the Standard toolbar or by clicking Tools, then clicking Spelling. When PowerPoint stops at a word that is misspelled, click the correctly spelled word from within the Suggestions, so that it becomes the "Change To" word, and then click the Change button. If PowerPoint stops at a word that is actually spelled correctly but that it doesn't recognize, click the Ignore button.
12. View the entire presentation in Slide Show mode.
13. Use the Save command to save the presentation to the Student Disk.
14. Print the outline of the presentation.
15. Close the file.

Open the file T2FILE2.PPT, save the file as S2FILE3.PPT, and do the following:

16. Change the template. Choose any template you think looks best.
17. In slide 1, change the text of the name of the author ("Angelena Cristenas") to another color.
18. In the title of slide 2, change "Goal and Objective," to "Objectives".
19. In slide 5, change the title to "Restructuring is Best".
20. E Also in slide 5, change the size of the font in the title from 44 to 60 points.

E 21. Insert a new slide between slides 1 and 2 by doing the following: Move the insertion point anywhere within the text of slide 1 in Outline view, then click the Insert New Slide button on the Standard toolbar. (You can also click Insert, then click New Slide.)

22. With the insertion point to the right of the slide icon for the new Slide 2, type the title, "Vision Statement".

23. For the main text in the new slide 2, type the text of the first bulleted item: "Inca Imports can become the premier produce import company in Southern California". Then type the text of the second bulleted item: "Inca Import can triple sales in the next two years".

24. In the new slide 2, change the color of the words "premier" and "triple" to yellow.

25. Edit the main text you added to slide 2 to follow the 6×6 rule as closely as possible.

E 26. Check the spelling within the presentation by using the Spelling button on the Standard toolbar or by clicking Tools, then clicking Spelling. When PowerPoint stops at a word that is misspelled, click the correctly spelled word from within the Suggestions, so that it becomes the "Change To" word, and then click the Change button. If PowerPoint stops at a word that is actually spelled correctly but that it doesn't recognize, click the Ignore button.

27. View the entire presentation in Slide Show mode.

28. Use the Save command to save the presentation to the Student Disk.

29. Print a copy of the outline of the presentation.

30. Save the file.

Case Problems

1. New Weave Fashions

Shaunda Shao works for New Weave Fashions, a clothing supplier for specialty retail stores in the northwest. New Weave contracts with wholesale fashion centers to supply New Weave retailers with women's shoes, sports fashions, and boutique merchandise. Shaunda's job is to provide training for New Weave's fledgling retailers.

Open the file P2NWEAVE.PPT, save the file as S2NWEAVE.PPT and do the following:

1. Change the template. Choose the one you think looks best.
2. Increase the font size of the title of slide 1 from 44 to 72 points.
3. In the first bulleted item in slide 2, use cut and paste to move the year ("1993") from the end of the line of text to the beginning, delete the word "in" that now appears at the end of the line, and change "Sales" to "sales".
4. In the second bulleted item in slide 2, use drag and drop to move "increased only 5.5%" from the middle of the line to the end of the line of text.
5. In slide 4, divide the second item into two separate items, and then revise the results so that they become "Obtaining volume discounts," and "Obtaining quick, reliable delivery".
6. Also in slide 4, move the last item ("Competing with well-known stores") so it becomes the second item in the main text of slide 2.
7. In slide 6, promote the phrase "Telephone follow-ups" so that it is on the same level as the bulleted item above it.

E 8. Change the color of title of slide 1 to yellow. Hint: When you click the Text Color button on the Formatting toolbar, yellow might not appear there, so click Other color, then click one of the yellow colored tiles.

E 9. Check the spelling within the presentation by using the Spelling button on the Standard toolbar or by clicking Tools, then clicking Spelling. When PowerPoint stops at a word that is misspelled, click the correctly spelled word from within the Suggestions, so that it becomes the "Change To" word, and then click the Change button. If PowerPoint stops at a word that is actually spelled correctly but that it doesn't recognize, click the Ignore button.
10. Use Slide Show to view all the slides of the presentation.
11. Save the file.
12. Print the outline of the presentation.
13. Print the presentation in black and white.
14. Close the file.

2. InfoTech

Pratt Deitschmann is seeking venture capital in the amount of $2.5 million for his startup company, InfoTech. InfoTech provides mailroom, word processing, in-house printing, and other information-output services for large corporations and law practices. Pratt has created a presentation to give to executives at A.B. O'Dair & Company, a New York City investment banking firm.

Open the file P2INFO.PPT, save the file as S2INFO.PPT, and do the following:

1. Change the font of the title of slide 1 to a sans serif font, such as Arial or Futura.
2. Change the size of the title from 44 to 54 points.
3. Delete "and Objective" from the title of slide 2.
4. Delete the first item of the main text of slide 4.
5. In slide 4, promote the four items that are double-indented to single-indented, so that all items in the main text are at the same level.
6. In slide 4, change the color of the phrase "5% lower" to yellow.
7. In slide 5, move the second item of the main text to become the third (last) item.
8. Move slide 5 so it becomes slide 6.
9. In slide 7, use drag and drop to move the text and make other changes so that the first item becomes "Initial venture capital of $2.5 million".
10. Use Slide Show mode to view the entire presentation.
11. Save the file using the current filename.
12. Print the slides (in black and white) and the outline of the presentation.
13. Close the file.

3. Team One Facilities Management

Virgil Pino works for Team One Facilities Management, a company that manages municipal waste disposal facilities. Virgil must communicate the unfortunate news that escalating travel costs threaten Team One's profitability. Do the following:

1. Close any presentation that might be in the PowerPoint presentation window.
2. **E** Begin a new presentation by clicking the New button on the Standard toolbar, clicking Pick a Look wizard, and clicking OK on the New Presentation dialog box. Follow the steps in the Pick a Look Wizard, making the selections as follows:
   a. Step 2: select On-Screen Presentation.
   b. Step 3: select the More button, then select the Travels template (travels.ppt)
   c. Step 4: select all the items.
   d. Step 5 (Slide Options): select Name, company or other text, type the shortened name of the company ("Team One") in place of whatever happens to be in the text box, and select Page Number.
   e. Steps 6–8 (Notes Options, Handout Options, Outline Options): keep the defaults.
   f. Step 9: click the Finish button.
3. Make sure you're in Slide view, then with the new slide 1 on the screen, type the title, "Rescuing Our Road Warriors", and type in the subtitle area the name of the author, "Virgil Pino".
4. **E** Virgil has already created some of the text for other slides, so insert the file P2TEAM.PPT into the current presentation. Hint: Click Insert, click Slides from File, and select p2team.ppt from the Student Disk.
5. With slide 2 ("Our Situation") in the presentation window in Slide view, change the word "profitability" in the last bulleted item from black to yellow.
6. In slide 3, add a new bulleted item between the last and the next-to-the-last items. Type the text of the item, "Cost per trip increased by 30%".
7. **E** Insert a new slide 4, and from the New Slide dialog box, choose the AutoLayout named "Bulleted list," located on the first row, second column of the AutoLayout box, and click the OK button. Make the title of the slide "Alternatives Considered". Type the following four items in the main text of the slide:
   a. Decrease amount of travel
   b. Decrease travel costs
   c. Increase other means of networking
   d. Increase efficiency of each trip
8. In slide 5, delete the item, "Coordinate trips to visit more clients per trip."
9. Switch to Outline view, and promote the item "Vision for the Future" so that it becomes the title of slide 6.
10. **E** Change the fonts of the title and of the main text in slides 2 through 5 so that they are the same as slides 1 and 6. Hint: Click the text in slide 6 and then read the Format toolbar to determine the font and font size in the title and in the main text, then apply those fonts to slides 2 through 4.
11. In slide 6, move the first item in the main text so it becomes the last item.
12. Add a new slide 7, selecting with the title "Summary" and with the bulleted items, "Change to meet growth", "Overcome the efficiency gap", "Manage travel time and money better", and "Rescue our road warriors".

E 13. Create a new slide 8 while still in Outline view. Then go into Slide view and change the Slide Layout to "Blank" (which is the last master style in the Slide Layout dialog box). Hint: To change a slide layout, click Format, click Slide Layout, scroll to the end of the box containing images of layout types and click the very last item, then click the Apply button.

14. Save the presentation using the filename S2TEAM.PPT.

15. Print the slides in black and white.

16. Close the file.

TUTORIAL 3

Creating Graphics for Your Slides

OBJECTIVES

In this tutorial you will:

- Resize and move text boxes and graphics boxes
- Change the general layout of an existing slide
- Insert pictures and clip-art images
- Create graphs and organizational charts
- Draw and manipulate graphic shapes

CASE

Sales Presentation Using the information gathered previously on customers of Inca Imports International, Enrique Hoffmann, director of marketing, and his staff have identified other businesses in the Southern California area that fit the profile of potential new customers. Enrique and his staff will focus their marketing efforts at these retail customers, who would benefit from having a wide range of fresh produce, year-round availability, and good customer service. Enrique and his staff are ready to prepare a presentation for these prospective clients.

In this tutorial you will create portions of Enrique's presentation, adding graphics to the text that Enrique has already written. A **graphic** is a picture, clip art, graph, chart, or table that you can add to a slide.

DESIGN PRINCIPLE WINDOW

USING GRAPHICS EFFECTIVELY

You should use graphics in the following situations:

- To present information that words can't communicate effectively
- To interest and motivate the reader
- To communicate relationships quickly
- To increase understanding and retention

Planning the Presentation

The marketing staff begins by planning their presentation:

- **Purpose for the presentation**: To convince business owners who do not now buy from Inca Imports to start buying our products and services
- **Type of presentation**: A 45-minute sales presentation
- **Audience**: Retail buyers and other business representatives
- **Location of presentation**: A conference room at the offices of Inca Imports
- **Audience needs**: To recognize their need for Inca's products and services and to understand how Inca Imports differs from other produce suppliers
- **Format**: One speaker presenting an electronic slide show consisting of five to seven slides

Manually Changing the Text Layout

After planning the presentation, Enrique and his staff created slides containing only text, knowing that they will need to add graphics to make the presentation more effective. Let's launch PowerPoint and open the current draft of Enrique's presentation.

To open an existing presentation and save it with a new name:

1. Launch PowerPoint and close the Tip of the Day dialog box if necessary. The PowerPoint startup dialog box appears on the screen. You will now retrieve the presentation that Enrique has created using the AutoContent Wizard.
2. Make sure the PowerPoint Student Disk is in drive A or B, then click the **Open Existing Presentation button** in the PowerPoint startup dialog box, and click the **OK Button** or press **[Enter]**. The Open dialog box appears on the screen.

   TROUBLE? If the PowerPoint startup dialog box does not appear on your screen, click the Open button on the Standard toolbar to display the Open dialog box.
3. Click the **Down Arrow** to the right of the Drives box, then click **a:** or **b:** (whichever drive contains your Student Disk).
4. Click **c3file1.ppt** in Files list box, and then click the **OK button**. The file C3FILE1.PPT appears in the presentation window. See Figure 3-1.

As you can see, PowerPoint displays an outline, consisting of Enrique's title slide (slide 1) and six additional slides. Now let's save the presentation using a different filename so that Enrique's original presentation file remains undisturbed.

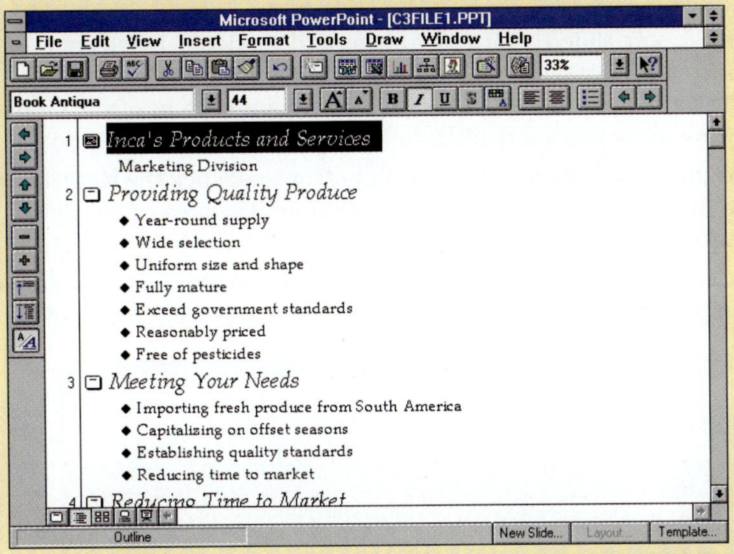

Figure 3-1
Presentation in the presentation window

❺ Click **File**, then click **Save As** to open the Save As dialog box.

❻ Make sure the drive containing your Student Disk is in the Drives list box, then edit the current filename to become **s3file1** and click the **OK button** or press **[Enter]**.

The Summary Info dialog box appears on the screen, with the information that Enrique typed previously.

❼ Click the **OK button** or press **[Enter]**. PowerPoint saves the presentation to the disk with the new filename.

Enrique is satisfied with his outline, and he is ready to add graphics to the slide. To do this, he will work in Slide view, which allows him to view and modify the position, size, and alignment of text boxes and graphics. **Text boxes** are the regions of the slide that contain text. Text boxes and graphics are objects. An **object** is any item (text box, clip art, graph, organization chart, picture) on a slide that you can move, resize, rotate, or otherwise manipulate.

Enrique first wants to add the company logo to the title slide. A company logo is a visual identification for the company. Enrique needs to make room for the logo by moving the three text boxes on the slide.

REFERENCE WINDOW

Resizing and Moving an Object

- Click anywhere on the object to select it. Resize handles appear around the object box (except for text boxes). For a text box, click the edge of the box to display the resize handles.
- Drag a resize handle to change the size of the object.
- Drag the object (for a text box, use the edge of the box) to a new location to move the object.

Let's rearrange the text boxes so that the logo will fit on the left side of the slide.

To resize and move text on a slide:

1. Make sure slide 1, "Inca's Products and Services," is selected (or the insertion point is somewhere within the text of slide 1) in Outline view, then click the **Slide View button**, on the View toolbar. PowerPoint switches from Outline view to Slide view. Now you are ready to select and rearrange the text boxes.
2. If the presentation window isn't maximized, click the **Maximize button** in the upper-right corner of the presentation window. The area of the slide is maximized so that you can see the entire slide.
3. Click anywhere in the text of the title "Inca's Products and Services." The text box appears. See Figure 3-2. Notice that the text is centered in the text box.

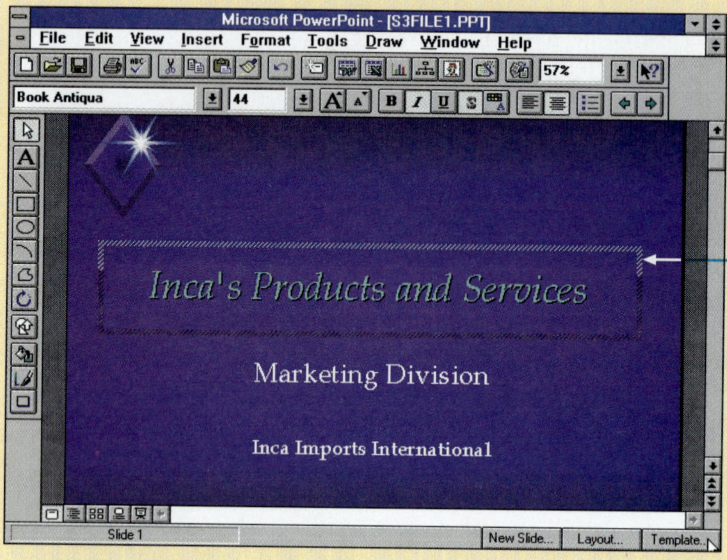

Figure 3-2
Selected text box

4. Click the edge of the text box. PowerPoint displays the resize handles around the text box. See Figure 3-3.

Figure 3-3
Selected text box with resize handles

TROUBLE? If, when you try to click the edge, the text box becomes deselected, click the text again, then click exactly on the box edge.

5. Position the mouse pointer over the resize handle in the lower-left corner of the text box. The pointer changes to ⤢.
6. Press and hold the mouse button so that the pointer changes to +, then drag the resize handle down and to the right to make the text box the approximate dimensions shown in Figure 3-4. Notice that a dotted outline of the text box follows the pointer movements. Don't worry about making the text box the exact same size and location as shown in the figure. Just resize it as closely as you can.

Figure 3-4
Resized text box

❼ Release the mouse button. The text is now on two lines instead of one line.

❽ Position the mouse pointer on the edge of the text box but *not* on a resize handle, then drag the text box up the screen to the approximate position shown in Figure 3-5.

Figure 3-5
Position of text box after dragging

Enrique now wants to align the text in the three boxes along their left margins and then move the text to the right. Let's do that now.

To align and move the text boxes:

❶ With the "Inca's Products" text box still selected, press and hold down **[Shift]**, click the other two text boxes, then release **[Shift]**.

As you can see, by holding down [Shift] while you click text on a slide, you can select more than one text box at a time. Notice that only the resize handles of the three text boxes are visible. You can modify all the selected text at once. First Enrique wants to change the text alignment so that it is aligned on the left side of the text boxes rather than centered, then he wants to align the text boxes themselves.

❷ Click the **Left Alignment button** on the Formatting toolbar. The text in each of the three text boxes becomes aligned on the left edge of its text box. Now you are ready to align the text boxes so their left edges are at the same horizontal position on the slide.

❸ Click **Draw**, click **Align**, and then click **Lefts**. The text boxes become aligned along their left edges.

❹ With all three text boxes still selected, position the mouse pointer on one of the text boxes, then drag the boxes to the right as far as they will go.

TROUBLE? If + appeared and the text boxes resize handles disappeared when you clicked the mouse button, you clicked outside of the text boxes. Select the text boxes again, then repeat Step 4.

As you can see, the "Marketing Division" text box is so large that you can't move the text very far to the right. Let's change the size of that text box, then try moving the slides again.

5. Click anywhere outside the text to deselect the three text boxes, then click the "Marketing Division" text box to select it, and click the edge to display the resize handles.
6. Drag the resize handle in the lower-right corner of the text box up and to the left to decrease the size of the box until it's just a little bigger than the text itself. You may have to scroll down a little to see the bottom of the text box.
7. Press and hold down **[Shift]**, click the other two text boxes so that all three text boxes are selected, then drag the text boxes to the right until they are positioned as shown in Figure 3-6.

Figure 3-6 Final position of the three text boxes

Having changed the size, position, and alignment of the text boxes, Enrique is ready to insert the company logo into the slide.

Inserting a Picture into a Slide

Enrique now wants to insert the Inca Imports International logo, a computer-generated image of fruit. Enrique wants to insert the logo to the left of the text boxes.

REFERENCE WINDOW

Inserting a Picture into a Slide

- Click Insert, then click Picture to display the Picture dialog box.
- Select the desired picture file from the disk, then click the OK button.
- Move and resize the picture as desired.

Let's insert the logo now.

To insert a picture into a slide:

1. Click **Insert**, then click **Picture**. The Insert Picture dialog box appears on the screen.
2. Make sure the Student Disk is in the disk drive, and select drive **a:** (or whichever drive contains your Student Disk) from the Drives box.

3. Click **iiilogo.bmp** in the File Names list to select the Inca Imports International logo, and then click the **OK button** or press **[Enter]**. The picture appears in the middle of the slide. The picture remains selected, as you can see from the handles around the edge of the graphic.
4. With the logo still selected, drag the graphics box to the left of the text so that the bottom edge of the logo is aligned with the last line of text, as shown in Figure 3-7, then click anywhere outside the slide to deselect the picture.

   TROUBLE? If you accidentally resized the graphic rather than moved it, click Undo in the Edit menu.

Figure 3-7
Completed slide 1

Enrique looks at his slide and feels that the background diamond shape doesn't go well with the logo, so he decides to eliminate the diamond.

5. Click **Format**, then click **Slide Background**. The Slide Background dialog box appears.
6. Click the **Display Objects on This Slide check box** at the top of the dialog box two times to deselect it. See Figure 3-8. This will delete the object, in this case, the diamond, from the slide background.

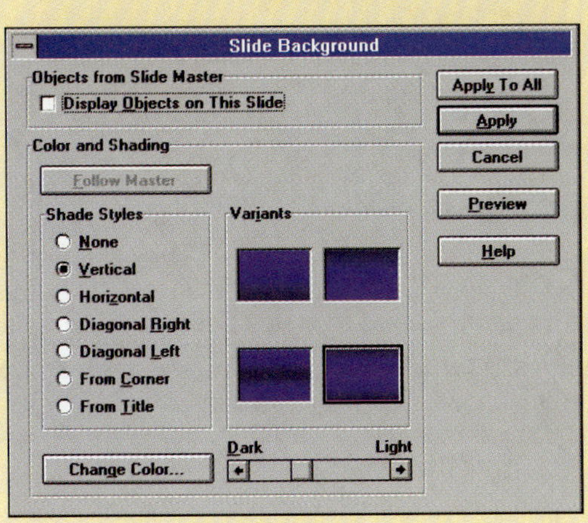

Figure 3-8

7. Click the **Apply button** (*not* the Apply to All button). The diamond no longer appears on the slide. That completes the work on this slide.
8. Click the **Next Slide button** at the bottom of the vertical scroll bar to view slide 2.

You are ready to work on slide 2 of Enrique's presentation.

Changing the Layout Using AutoLayout

Enrique wants to add an item to the bulleted list in slide 2, "Providing Quality Produce." He decides that with the addition of this item, the bulleted list will be too long to fit on the slide. The slide might look better with two columns. He could reformat the slide manually, but he decides to use an AutoLayout.

REFERENCE WINDOW

Changing the Layout of a Slide

- Get into Slide view and then move to (display) the slide whose layout you want to change.
- Click the Layout button in the status bar to display the Slide Layout dialog box.
- Click the layout that corresponds to the desired slide layout, and then click the Reapply button.

Let's change the layout of the slide now to accommodate a second column of text.

To change the layout of an existing slide:

1. Click the **Layout button** in the status bar. PowerPoint displays the Slide Layout dialog box. See Figure 3-9.

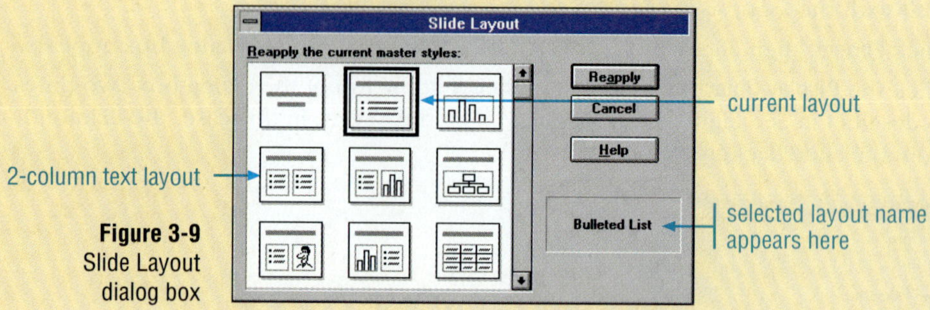

Figure 3-9 Slide Layout dialog box

2. Click the layout with the **2 Column Text** layout.

   TROUBLE? If you're not sure which is the 2 Column Text layout, click each picture until the box at the lower right of the dialog box displays the name "2 Column Text." On most computers, it is the picture in the second row, first column, as shown in Figure 3-9.

3. Click the **Apply button**. PowerPoint reformats the slide, with a new text box on the right. See Figure 3-10.

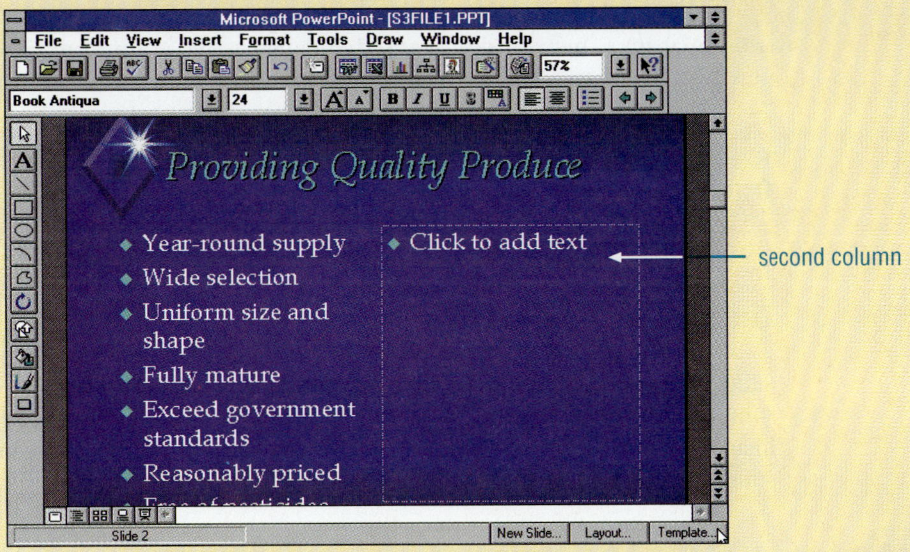

Figure 3-10
New layout of slide 2

Enrique is ready to add the new final item to the bulleted list.

To add text to a new text box:

❶ Click anywhere within the text box that says, "**Click to add text.**" PowerPoint removes the message that was in the text box, displays a bullet, and positions the insertion point to the right of the bullet.

❷ Type **Hand picked** and press **[Enter]**.

Now Enrique wants to move the last three items in the first column to the end of the second column so the columns are balanced.

❸ Click anywhere on the text in the first column. The text box becomes selected.

❹ Scroll down so you can see the last three items in the first column.

❺ Position the mouse pointer over the bullet next to "Exceed government standards." The mouse pointer changes to ✥.

❻ Click the mouse button, press and hold **[Shift]**, click the bullets next to "Reasonably priced" and "Free of pesticides," then release **[Shift]**.

❼ Click the **Cut button** on the Standard toolbar. The text disappears from the screen and is moved to the Clipboard.

❽ Press **[Backspace]** to delete the fifth bullet in the first column.

❾ Click I just after the second bullet in the second column, then click the **Paste button** on the Standard toolbar. The three cut items appear in the second column. See Figure 3-11.

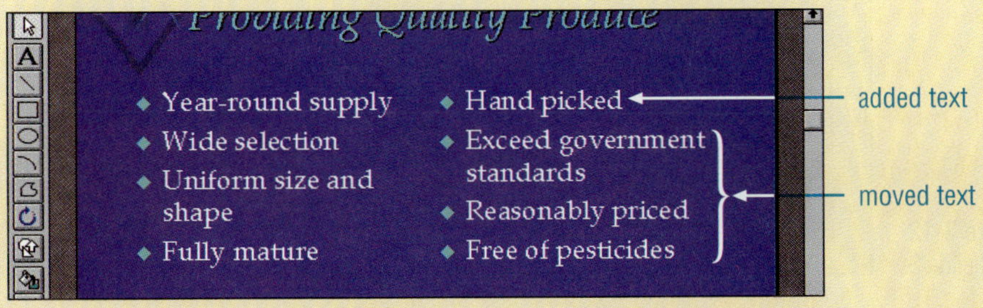

Figure 3-11
Completed slide 2

You have completed slide 2 of Enrique's presentation. The slide now contains the additional text that Enrique wanted and has a two-column design to accommodate the new text in an attractive and readable way. Enrique now wants to look at slide 3.

To move to the next slide:

❶ Click the **Next Slide button** at the bottom of the vertical scroll bar.

Inserting Clip Art

Slide 3, "Meeting Your Needs," has four items of information. Enrique wants to include some clip art to add interest to this slide. In PowerPoint, **clip art** specifically refers to images in the Microsoft Clip Art Gallery, whereas **picture** is any image from some other source, including clip-art libraries supplied by other companies.

DESIGN PRINCIPLE WINDOW

Selecting an Appropriate Type of Graphic

- Consider your audience: job, experience, education, culture
- Consider your purpose: to inform, persuade, instruct, identify, interest, motivate
- Consider the type of information on the slide: numerical values, logical relationships, procedures and processes, visual and spatial characteristics

Let's now change the layout of the slide and add clip art to it.

To change the layout of the slide and add clip art:

❶ Click the **Layout button** in the status bar to display the Slide Layout dialog box, click the layout with the description of **Text & Clip Art**, then click the **Apply button** to change the layout of the slide. See Figure 3-12.

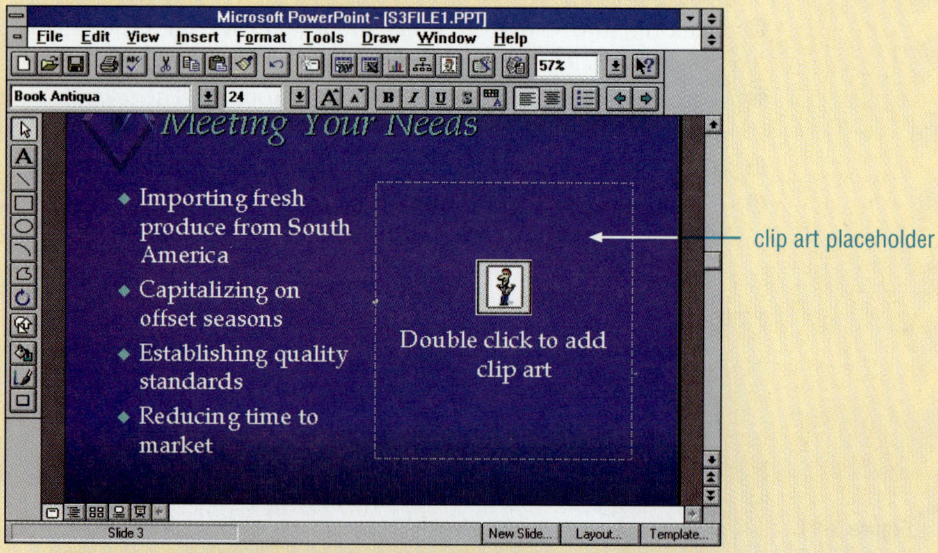

Figure 3-12
New layout of slide 3

❷ Double-click the box labeled **"Double click to add clip art."** PowerPoint displays the Microsoft Clip Art Gallery dialog box. See Figure 3-13.

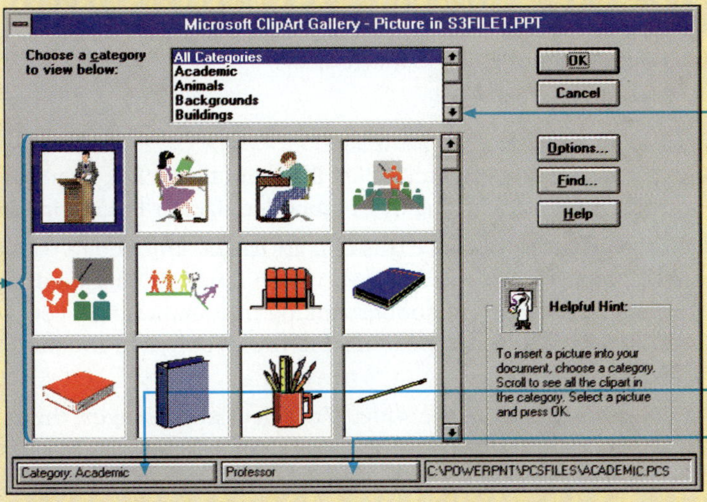

Figure 3-13 Microsoft Clip Art Gallery dialog box

TROUBLE? If PowerPoint displays a dialog box with the question, "Would you like to add clip art from PowerPoint now?," click the Yes button and then wait for PowerPoint to set up its built-in clip-art library.

❸ Scroll the "Choose a category to view below" list box until you see "People," then click **People** to select that category.

TROUBLE? If you don't see a list of categories for the clip-art library, or if the clip art is missing altogether, consult your technical support person or instructor. If you do have clip art to choose from, but you don't have the People category, choose any clip art you prefer in order to complete these steps.

❹ Scroll the clip-art images within the People category until you see the image of two men standing by a world map, then click that image. See Figure 3-14. The clip-art title at the bottom of the dialog box gives the name of the image, "World Map and Men."

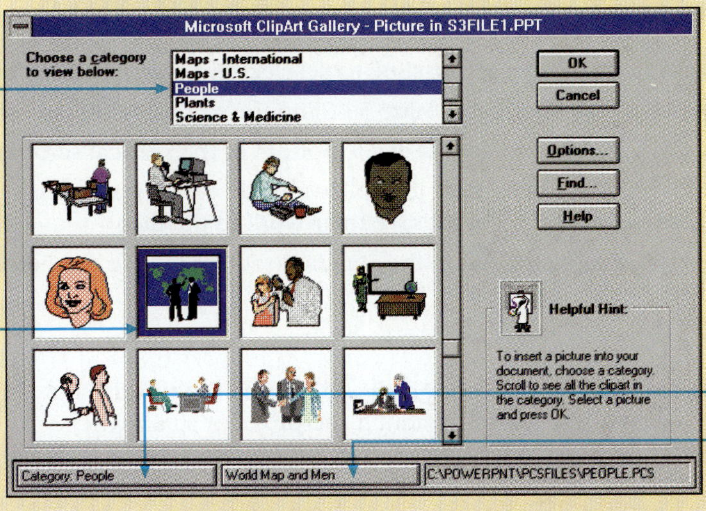

Figure 3-14 Clip-art images with World Map and Men selected

❺ Click the **OK button**. The clip art is inserted into the slide.

Enrique would like the men to point to South America rather than to Africa. To do this, he will ungroup the image into individual objects, then move the object comprising the men to a new location relative to the map object. To **ungroup** means to convert a single image into smaller, individual objects.

Let's ungroup and edit the image now.

To ungroup and edit the clip art image:

1. With the image still selected, click **Draw** and then click **Ungroup**. PowerPoint displays a warning about discarding any embedded data or linking information.
2. Click the **OK button**, because this clip art has no embedded data or linking information. (A graph from a spreadsheet, which might be modified if you change the spreadsheet data, would contain linking information that you wouldn't want to break.) Resize handles appear around the two men in the picture as well as around the world map.
3. Click in a blank area of the slide to deselect both images, then click one of the men in the clip art. The image of the men becomes selected, but not the world map.

   TROUBLE? If you didn't use the World Map and Men clip-art image, your image may not be able to ungroup, or if it does ungroup, you may not be able to individually select one of the items. If this occurs, skip to the next section, "Inserting a Graph."
4. Drag the men to the left and down so that they point to the northern part of South America, as shown in Figure 3-15. To position the selected image more precisely, press [↓], [↑], or [←] to move the image in very small increments.

Figure 3-15
Clip art after ungrouping and moving men

5. Click in a blank area of the slide to deselect the image of the men.

   You have now completed slide 3 of Enrique's presentation.
6. Click the **Next Slide button** at the bottom of the vertical scroll bar.

   Enrique and the marketing group have made considerable edits to the presentation, so they decide they should save their work to the disk.
7. Click the **Save button** on the Standard toolbar to save the current version of S3FILE1.PPT to the disk.

If you want to take a break and resume the tutorial at a later time, you can do so now. If you exit PowerPoint, launch the program again when you want to resume working, open the presentation file S3FILE1.PPT, and make sure you are in Slide view looking at slide 4. Then continue with the next section.

Inserting a Graph

On slide 4 of his presentation, Enrique wants to add a column chart that compares Inca Imports International's time to market (that is, the time from picking to customer delivery, in hours) during the past four quarters with the other two major produce import companies in southern California.

REFERENCE WINDOW

Inserting a Column Chart

- Display the desired slide in Slide view.
- If necessary, change the Slide Layout to "Text & Graph" or "Graphic & Text."
- Double-click the area marked "Double click to add graph." PowerPoint displays a data sheet.
- Edit the information in the data sheet for the data that you want to plot.
- Click anywhere outside the data sheet, then click anywhere outside the graph box.

Let's add the graph now.

To add a column chart to the slide:

❶ Click the **Layout button** in the status bar, click the layout with the name **Text & Graph** (it's the picture in the second row in the second column), then click the **Apply button**. The text on the slide becomes formatted into a smaller text box on the left side of the slide, and a graphs box placeholder appears on the right side.

❷ Double-click the **graphs box placeholder**. After a minute or more, PowerPoint inserts a sample graph and displays a data sheet, similar to a spreadsheet such as Microsoft Excel or Lotus 1-2-3 in a window in the center of the screen.

TROUBLE? Don't worry if the colors on the slide become distorted. They'll return to normal once you close the data sheet window.

With the sample graph and data sheet on the screen, you simply change the information in the data sheet to create your own graph. The information on the data sheet is stored in **cells**, which are the little boxes that contain a number, word or phrase. The cells are organized into rows and columns. The rows are numbered 1, 2, 3. . ., whereas the columns are labeled A, B, C. . . . Enrique edits the information in the data sheet to reflect the three companies' times to market. Let's do that now.

To edit the information in the data sheet:

❶ Position the mouse pointer over the cell that contains the word "**East.**" The pointer changes to .

❷ Click the cell that contains the word "**East,**" and type **SCP** (which stands for "Southern California Produce," one of the major competitors of Inca Imports).

❸ Press[↓] to select the cell labeled **"West,"** then type **CCF** (which stands for "Central City Foods," the other major competitor of Inca Imports).

❹ Repeat Step 3 to replace **"North"** with **Inca**. See Figure 3-16. Now you're ready to change the actual numbers in the data sheet.

S3FILE1.PPT - Datasheet

		A	B	C	D
		1st Qtr	2nd Qtr	3rd Qtr	4th Qtr
1	SCP	20.4	27.4	90	20.4
2	CCF	30.6	38.6	34.6	31.6
3	Inca	45.9	46.9	45	43.9
4					

new labels

Figure 3-16 Data sheet after changing labels

❺ Click cell **A1**, the cell at which column A and row 1 intersect, then type **18**. This is the average time to market in hours of SCP during the first quarter of the year.

❻ Press **[Tab]** or [→] to select cell **B1**, type **27**, press **[Tab]**, type **22**, press **[Tab]**, then type **20**. This completes the data for SCP.

❼ Using the same procedure as in Steps 5 and 6, replace the current data for CCF and for Inca, using the figures shown in Figure 3-17. Carefully check the data sheet to make sure it matches Figure 3-17. Make any corrections necessary.

S3FILE1.PPT - Datasheet

		A	B	C	D
		1st Qtr	2nd Qtr	3rd Qtr	4th Qtr
1	SCP	18	27	22	20
2	CCF	30	38	34	32
3	Inca	16	18	17	16
4					

Figure 3-17 Completed data sheet

❽ Click anywhere outside the data sheet but still within the graph box (for example, in the lower-right corner of the graph box) to remove the data sheet from the screen. The completed graph appears on the screen.

Now Enrique wants to insert a title to label the vertical axis of his graph. Let's do that now.

To insert a title into a graph:

❶ Click **Insert**, then click **Titles**. PowerPoint displays the Titles dialog box.

❷ Click the **Value (Z Axis check box)**, then click the **OK button**. PowerPoint displays a small text box to the left of the vertical axis with the letter "Z" as its contents.

❸ Double-click one of the resize handles of the **Z-axis title**. The Format Axis Title dialog box appears on the screen. See Figure 3-18.

TROUBLE? If you clicked or double-clicked inside the text box, the resize handles disappear. Click within the graph box but outside of any other object in the box, for example, in the lower-right corner of the graph box, then double-click the Z-axis title. If the Format Plot Area dialog box appears as a result of Step 3, click the cancel button, then follow the steps described in this TROUBLE? paragraph.

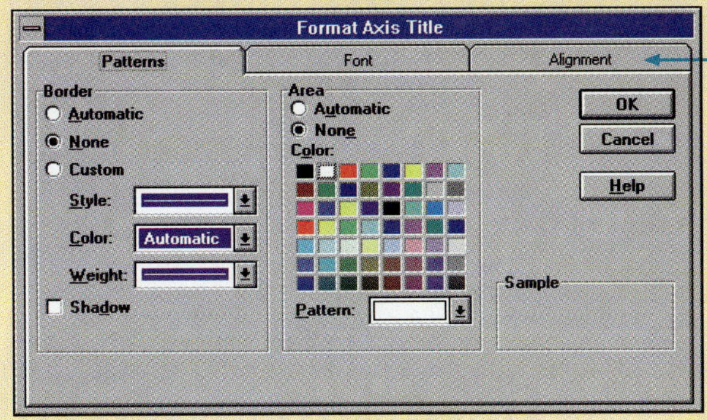

Figure 3-18
Format Axis Title dialog box

❹ Click the **Alignment** folder tab at the top of the dialog box, then in the Orientation box, click the "Text" with the vertical orientation (it reads bottom to top). It's the middle box in the row of three boxes.

❺ Click the **OK button** to return to the graph on the slide.

❻ Click on the **"Z"** in the Z-axis title, delete the Z (for example, by pressing **[Backspace]**), then type **Hours**. This indicates that graphed time from picking to delivery is in hours. Click anywhere within the graph box but outside of other objects to deselect the title.

Enrique notices that the word "2nd" on the X-axis label is split in two, so he decides to increase the width of the graph to allow more room for the text.

❼ Position the mouse pointer over the left center resize handle, wait a moment for the double-arrow pointer to appear, then drag the handle left until the left edge of the graph is near the right edge of the text of the slide. You may have to wait a minute while holding the mouse button before the box will actually resize. See Figure 3-19.

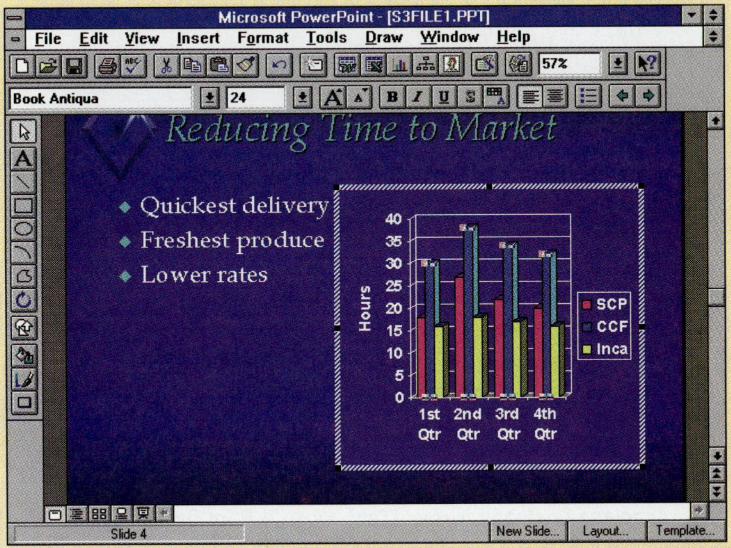

Figure 3-19
Completed graph in slide 4

TROUBLE? If your graph doesn't look like Figure 3-19, click the View Datasheet button in the Graph toolbar to display the data sheet. Make the necessary revisions by comparing your data sheet with Figure 3-17.

You have now completed slide 4 of Enrique's presentation. Let's deselect the graph and go to the next slide.

To deselect the graph and advance to the next slide:

1. Click twice outside the graph area, once to exit the graph and once to deselect the graph.
2. Click the **Next Slide button** on the vertical scroll bar.

Inserting an Organization Chart

Because Inca Imports is a fairly new company, Enrique and his staff feel that it's important for potential clients to understand the high level of experience of Inca employees in the import and produce businesses. Enrique decides that an organization chart will communicate this information better than a bulleted list. Let's create the organization chart now.

To create an organization chart:

1. Click the **Insert Org Chart button** on the Standard toolbar. After a few moments, the Microsoft Organization Chart window appears on the screen with the Organization Chart toolbar across the top.
2. Click the **Maximize button** on the Organization Chart window to make it cover the entire screen. See Figure 3-20. A chart with text placeholders is in the window. The chart has two levels of organization. The first box, at the top of the chart, is already selected, as you can tell from its black background. When you start typing, the text will appear in that selected box.

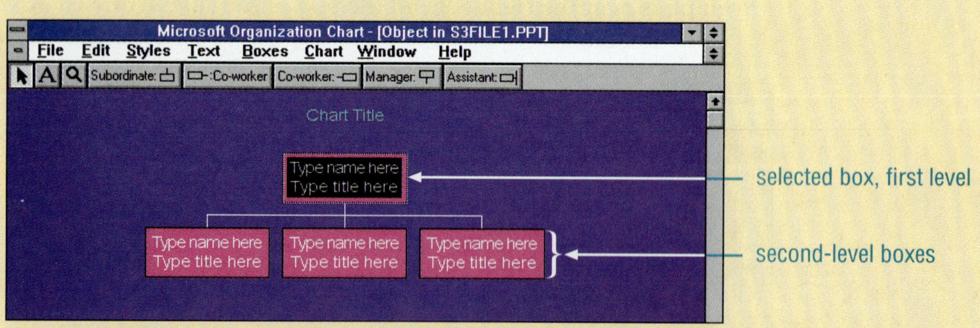

Figure 3-20 Microsoft Organization Chart window

3. Type **Patricia Cuevas.** As soon as you started typing, the box expanded to display four lines.
4. Press **[Tab]** or **[Enter]**. The placeholder text "Type title here" becomes selected.
5. Type **President**, press **[Tab]**, and type **13 years experience**. This completes the first box.
6. Click the second-level box on the left side. The box becomes selected, as shown by its black background.
7. Type **Angelena Cristenas**, press **[Tab]**, type **V.P. of Operations**, press **[Tab]**, and type **13 years experience**. This completes the text of that text box in the organization chart.
8. Using the same procedure as in Steps 6 and 7, complete the other two boxes of the organization chart, so that they contain the text shown in Figure 3-21, then click anywhere within the Microsoft Organization Chart window but outside of any text or organization box.

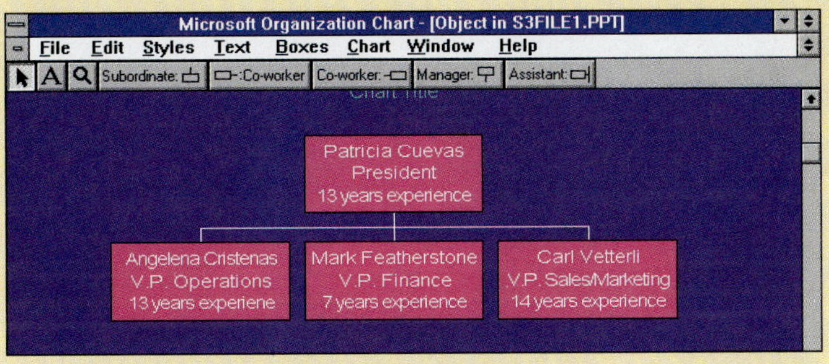

Figure 3-21
First two levels of organization chart

9. If you made any typing errors, click the box containing the error, then press **[Tab]** until the line containing the error is highlighted, then retype that line.

You have completed the first two levels of the organization chart. Enrique also wants to show the experience personnel at Inca Imports have in handling produce and responding to customer delivery needs. The customer service employees work under Angelena Cristenas. Let's add the new levels of organization now.

To add subordinate levels to an organization chart:

1. Click the **Subordinate button** Subordinate: on the Organization Chart toolbar. The mouse pointer changes to ⊥.
2. Click the box containing "Angelena Cristenas." A new organization level appears below Angelena's box. See Figure 3-22. The small black box within the new box indicates that the new box is selected and ready for you to type new text.

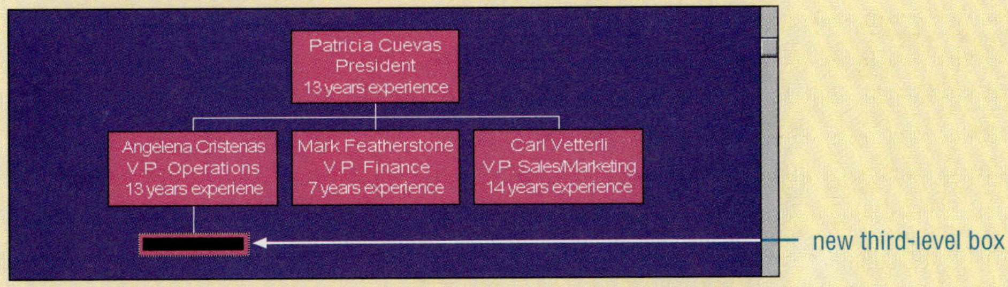

Figure 3-22
New organization level

3. Type **Carlos Becerra**. As soon as you begin to type, the other text placeholders appear in the box.
4. Press **[Tab]**, type **QA Manager**, press **[Tab]**, and type **22 years experience**. This completes the box for Carlos Becerra, QA (quality assurance) manager.
5. Click Subordinate: and click the box containing "Carlos Becerra" to add a subordinate box underneath Carlos.
6. Type **Norma Lopez**, press **[Tab]**, type **Customer Service**, press **[Tab]**, and type **8 years experience**, then click anywhere in the Organization Chart window but outside of any text or box. Your chart should now look like Figure 3-23.

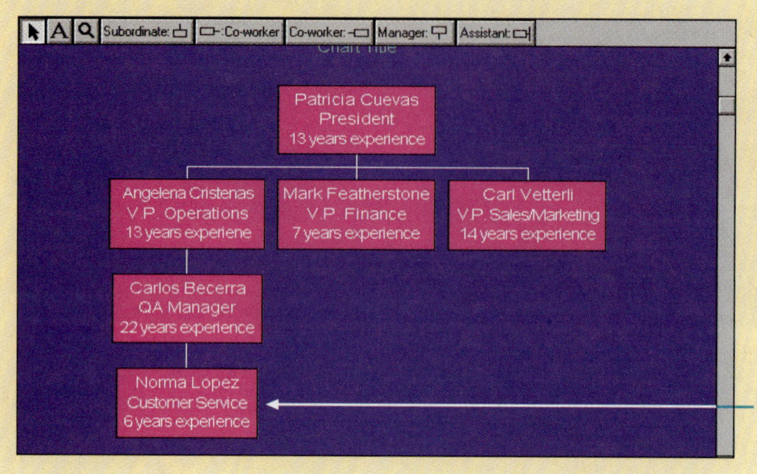

Figure 3-23
Chart after adding a subordinate box

Enrique decides to add a coworker to the chart. Let's do it now.

To add a coworker to an organization chart:

1. Click the right **Coworker button** on the Organization Chart toolbar. The mouse changes to ─▭. This allows you to add a coworker box to the right of an existing box.
2. Click the box containing **"Norma Lopez"** to add a new box to its right, type **Juanita Rojas**, press **[Tab]**, type **Manager, Quito Center**, press **[Tab]**, type **3 years experience**, and click anywhere in the window but outside of any box or text.

You have completed the organization chart. You now have to exit the Organization Chart window and add the organization chart to the slide.

To exit the Organization Chart window and add the chart to the slide:

1. Click **File**, then click **Exit and return to S3FILE1.PPT**. A dialog box appears on the screen asking if you want to update the object. The object in this case is the new organizational chart.
2. Click the **Yes button**. After looking over the organization chart, Enrique thinks it should be bigger.
3. Drag the resize handle in the upper-left corner up and to the left, and drag the resize handle in the lower-right corner down and to the right until the organization chart is approximately the size shown in Figure 3-24.

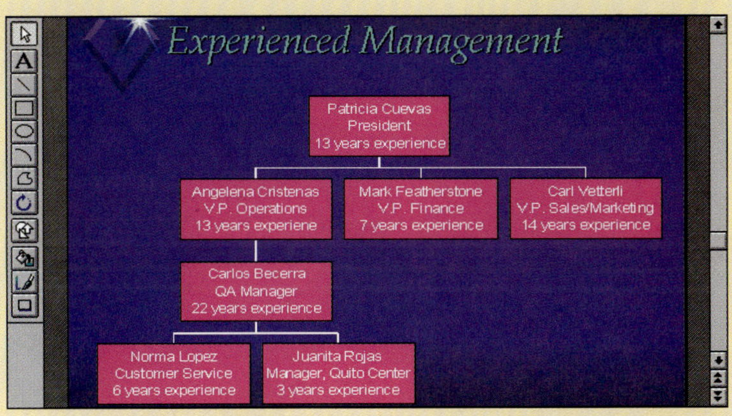

Figure 3-24 Completed organization chart in slide 5

❹ Click anywhere outside the selected organization chart to deselect it. Slide 5 now looks like Figure 3-24.

This completes the five current slides in Enrique's presentation. However, he has decided to add one more slide to the presentation.

❺ Click the **Next Slide button** on the vertical scroll bar.

If you want to take a break and resume the tutorial at a later time, you can do so now. If you exit PowerPoint, launch the program again when you want to resume working, open the presentation file S3FILE1.PPT, and make sure you are in Slide view looking at slide 6. Then continue with the next section.

Creating and Manipulating a Shape

Enrique wants to add a simple drawing with text to slide 6 to demonstrate the three major benefits of the company. To do this, Enrique wants to insert an inverted triangle onto slide 6. Let's do that now.

To insert a shape onto a slide:

❶ Click the **AutoShapes button** on the Drawing toolbar. PowerPoint displays the AutoShapes palette.

❷ Click the **Isosceles Triangle Tool button** on the AutoShapes palette. The mouse pointer changes to the cross-bar pointer.

❸ Position + an inch below the first "n" in "International" (in the title of the slide), then drag down and to the right. The outline of a triangle appears as you drag.

❹ Release the mouse button when your triangle is approximately the same size as the one in Figure 3-25.

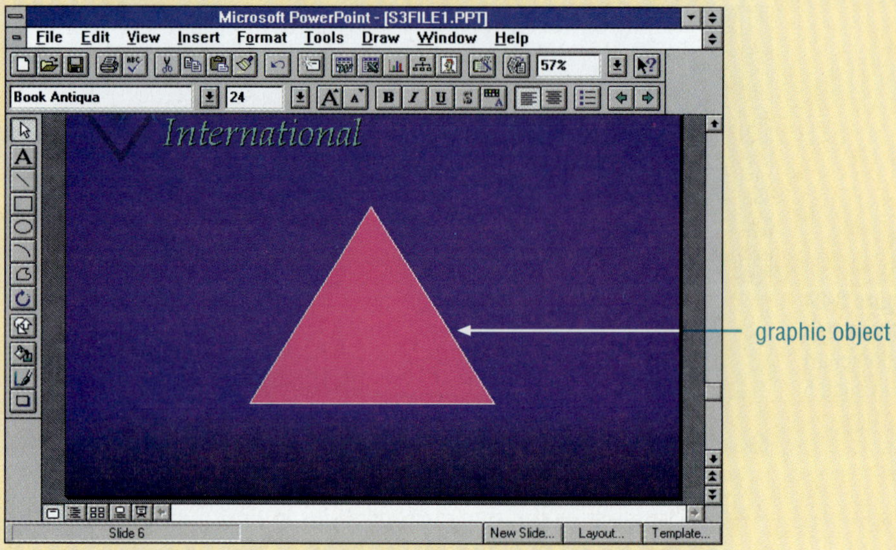

Figure 3-25 Slide with drawn triangle

5. Click the **Control menu box** in the upper-left corner of the AutoShapes palette to close the palette. It disappears from the screen. See Figure 3-25.

   TROUBLE? If your triangle doesn't look similar the one in Figure 3-25, you can move your triangle by dragging it to a new location; you can resize or change the shape of your triangle by dragging one or more of the resize handles; or you can press [Backspace] to completely delete your triangle, then repeat Steps 1 through 5 to redraw the triangle.

   Notice that the default color of the drawn object is pink. Enrique decides that pink is too bright for his presentation, and changes the color of the triangle.

6. Click **Format**, then click **Colors and Lines**. The Colors and Lines dialog box appears on the screen.

7. Click the **Down arrow** in the Fill box, and click the **cyan (blue-green) tile**, then click the **OK button**.

The triangle is the desired size and color, but Enrique decides he wants to flip the triangle so it is pointing down instead of up. Let's flip the triangle now.

To flip an object:

1. Make sure the triangle is still selected.
2. Click **Draw** on the Menu bar, then click **Rotate/Flip**, and click **Flip Vertical**.
3. Click in a blank region of the slide to deselect the triangle.

   Your triangle should be positioned, colored, sized, and oriented similar to the one shown in Figure 3-26.

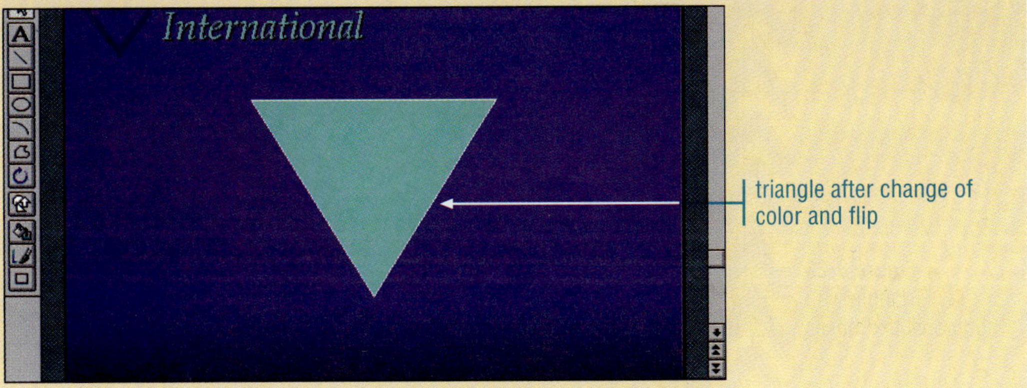

Figure 3-26 Final position, size, color, and orientation of triangle

Adding a Text Box

Enrique is ready to add the text naming the three benefits of Inca Imports on each side of the triangle. Let's do that now.

To add a text box to the slide:

❶ Click the **Text Tool button** A on the Drawing toolbar. The mouse pointer changes to ↓.

❷ Move the mouse pointer so it is just above the upper-left corner of the triangle and click at that position. PowerPoint creates a small empty text box, with the insertion point inside.

❸ Type **Quality Produce**.

❹ Click anywhere on the edge of the text box to select it.

❺ Drag the edge of the text box until it is positioned just above and centered on the upper edge of the triangle, as shown in Figure 3-27.

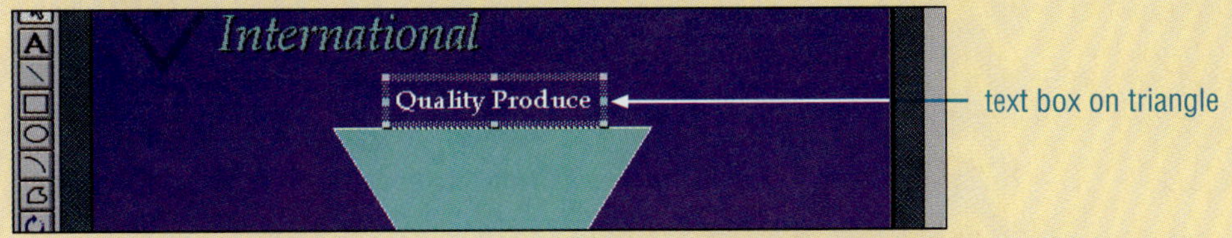

Figure 3-27 Triangle with first text box

❻ Click A, then click ↓ to the right of the triangle and type **Year-round Service**.

❼ Click A, then click ↓ to the left of the triangle and type **Satisfied Customers**. Click in a blank area of the slide to deselect the text box. Your slide should now look similar to Figure 3-28. Don't worry if the text you added to the sides of the triangle is not in the same position as in the figure. You will move it in the next set of steps.

Figure 3-28
Triangle with additional text boxes

Now you'll rotate the text boxes to make them parallel to the sides of the triangle. The method for rotating text is similar to rotating graphics (or rotating any other object).

To rotate and move the text boxes:

1. Select the text box that contains "**Year-round Service**" by clicking anywhere within the box then clicking the edge of the box. The resize handles appear around the box.
2. Click the **Free Rotate Tool button** on the Drawing toolbar. The mouse pointer changes to ↻.
3. Position the ↻ over one of the resize handles (it doesn't matter which). The pointer changes again, this time to ⁘.
4. Press and hold the mouse button. The pointer changes a third time, this time to +.
5. Rotate the handle counterclockwise until the status bar indicates that you have rotated the box about 60 degrees or until the top edge of the box is parallel to the lower-right edge of the triangle. See Figure 3-29.

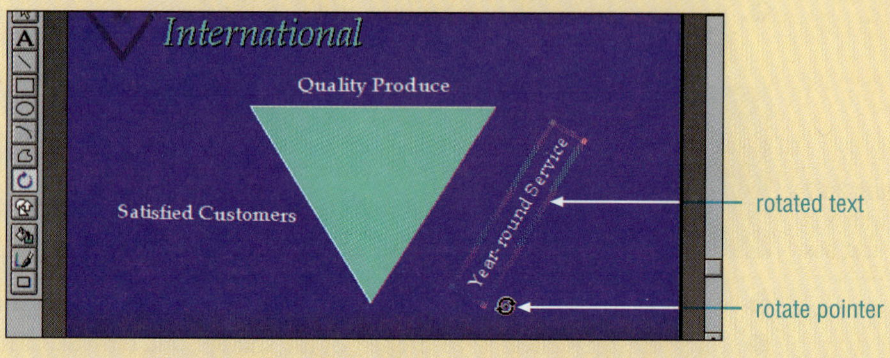

Figure 3-29
Slide after rotating text

6. Click the **Selection Tool button** on the Drawing toolbar, then select the "**Year-round Service**" text box. The first time you click the text, it flips so it is horizontal again. After you click the edge of the text box to select it, the text returns to its rotated position.
7. Drag the edge of the text box until it is close to and centered on the lower-right edge of the triangle.

8. Select the text box that contains "**Satisfied Customers,**" then repeat Steps 2 through 7, except this time rotate the box clockwise to about 300 degrees or until it is parallel to the lower-left edge of the triangle, and then position the text box so it is close to and centered on that edge of the triangle.
9. Deselect the text box. Your slide should look like Figure 3-30.

Figure 3-30
Completed slide 6

Enrique and his staff have now completed the entire presentation, so Enrique wants to save the final version to the disk.

10. With the Student Disk still in the disk drive, click the **Save button** on the Standard toolbar. PowerPoint saves the file using its current filename, S3FILE1.PPT.

A copy of the updated presentation is now on your Student Disk.

Viewing and Printing the Completed Slide Show

Enrique wants to view the completed slide show before he prints it.

To view the completed presentation as a slide show:

1. Press **[Ctrl][Home]** or drag the **elevator** to the top of the vertical scroll bar. This ensures that when you begin the Slide Show, slide 1 appears on the screen first.
2. Click the **Slide Show button** on the View toolbar to begin the slide show.
3. After you look at each slide, click the left mouse button or press the space bar to advance to the next slide. Continue advancing until you've seen the entire slide show and PowerPoint returns to Slide view.

Enrique and his staff want a hard copy of their presentation for their files, so they print the entire presentation. Let's print the presentation now.

To print the presentation:

1. Click **File**, then click **Print** to display the Print dialog box, then in the Print What box, select **Slides** if it's not already selected.

2. If you're using a black-and-white printer, click the **Pure Black & White checkbox** on the Print dialog box, and then click the **OK button** to print the slides. The Pure Black & White option speeds up printing because it doesn't print gray-scale objects. All text and graphics appear pure black or pure white.

3. If you desire, you may now exit PowerPoint.

■ ■ ■

Questions

1. Describe how to do the following:
   a. Select a text box so that resize handles appear
   b. Change the size of a text box
   c. Move a text box on a slide
   d. Change the alignment of a text box from center to left alignment
2. Write a list of steps required to do each of the following:
   a. Insert a picture into a slide
   b. Change the Layout of an existing slide
   c. Insert a Graph into a slide
   d. Insert an Organization Chart into a slide
   e. Add a slide to a presentation
   E f. Draw a circle on a slide. Hint: To draw a circle, use the Ellipse Tool while holding down [Shift]
3. List four situations in which you could use graphics effectively.
4. Why would you ungroup a clip-art image?
5. Explain the meaning of the following terms:
   a. Slide Layout
   b. clip art
   c. object
   d. Center Alignment
   e. data sheet
   f. organization chart
   g. subordinate box
   h. resize handles
6. What are two methods (one using the keyboard and the other using the mouse) for moving to (displaying) the first slide in a presentation while in Slide view?
7. How do you rotate an object (text box or graphics box)?
8. List three principles for selecting an appropriate type of graphic.
9. **E** Explain an advantage and disadvantage of moving a selected object (text box or graphics box) by dragging with the mouse or by pressing the arrow keys.
10. **E** List and describe the first nine tools (starting with Selection Tool) on the Drawing toolbar.

Tutorial Assignments

In the following Tutorial Assignments, make sure you click the Open an Existing File button when you launch PowerPoint or, if PowerPoint is already running, click the Open button on the Standard toolbar, and then open each file. After working with a presentation and saving your changes, close the presentation.

Open the file T3FILE1.PPT and do the following:

1. Save the file to your student disk as S3FILE2.PPT.
2. Make sure that PowerPoint is in Slide view and that slide 1 appears in the presentation window.
3. Decrease the size of each of the two text boxes so that they fit just around the text contained in each box.
4. Change the text in both text boxes to Left Alignment.
5. Insert the picture file IIILOGO.BMP into slide 1, decrease the size of the logo, then move the picture just to the right of the red bars in the upper-left corner of the slide. Try to align the top of the graphic with the top of the bars.
6. Move the two text boxes so that their left edges are directly beneath the left edge of the picture. Use the Draw, Align, Lefts command to align them precisely.
7. Change the layout of slide 2 to "2 Column Text."
8. In the right-hand column of slide 2, add the following three bulleted items: "Ad in food industry trade magazine," "Sample produce to interested businesses," "Complimentary shipment to large companies."
9. In slide 3 change the layout to "Clip Art & Text," so that the clip art is on the left and the text is on the right.
10. In the placeholder for the clip art in slide 3, add the image from the People category called "Man with Pad," which pictures a man standing up holding a small notepad. If your copy of PowerPoint doesn't have that clip-art image, use another one of your choice.
11. Add an organization chart to slide 4. Put Enrique Hoffmann, Director of Marketing, at the top of the chart. Add Melanie Zapatos and Samuel Clarke, both Marketing Managers, to the second level. Then, on the third level under Melanie Zapatos, add two Sales Representatives, Carlos Anderson and Ana Maria Prado; and under Samuel Clarke add two Sales Representatives, Gina Parker and Jesus Calderon. Hint: To delete an unwanted box on the organization chart, select the box, and then press [Backspace] or [Delete].

E 12. Add a new slide 5. Choose "Title Only" as the slide layout. Make the title of the slide "Marketing Process." Add text and AutoShapes to create a slide that looks like Figure 3-31. You may have to move, resize, and align text and graphics boxes to make the slide look right. Hint: To make the arrows the same size and shape, use AutoShapes to draw one of the arrows and then use the Copy and Paste buttons on the Standard toolbar to create the others. To align the centers of objects vertically (text boxes and graphics boxes), use the Draw, Align, Centers command.

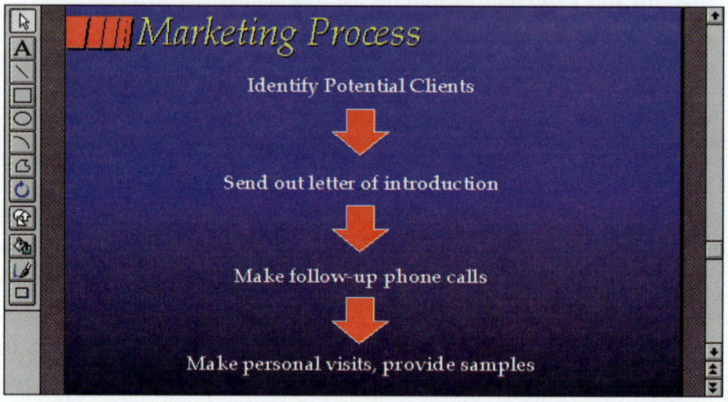

Figure 3-31

E 13. Add a new slide 6. Choose "Graph" as the slide layout. Make the title of the slide "Comparison of 4th Qtr Sales, 1992-95." Double-click the graph icon, and then in the data sheet, delete the second and thirds rows Hint: Click the gray box labeled 2, then click Edit, and click Delete to delete the entire row. Change labels in columns A through D from "1st Qtr," "2nd Qtr," and so forth, to "1992," "1993," "1994," and "1995." Change the label in that row from "East" to "4th Qtr Sales." Make the numbers in cells A1 through D1 the following: $420, $475, $710, $1025. Add the title "Thousands" to the Z-axis; make the title vertical, reading bottom to top. Close the data sheet and then deselect the graph.

E 14. Check the spelling within the presentation by clicking the Spelling button on the Standard toolbar or by clicking Tools, then clicking Spelling.

15. View the entire presentation in Slide Show view.
16. Save your changes, then print a copy of the slides of the presentation. Print them using the Black & White option if you don't have a color printer.
17. Close the file.

Open the file T3FILE2.PPT and do the following:

18. Save it to your Student Disk as S3FILE3.PPT.
19. Make sure that PowerPoint is in Slide view and that slide 1 appears in the presentation window.
20. Insert the picture file T3DESIGN.BMP from the Student Disk into slide 1, then position the picture below the author's name, "Norma Lopez."
21. Remove the Slide Master objects from this title slide.
22. Change the layout of slide 2 to "2 Column Text."
23. In the right-hand column of slide 2, add the following two bulleted items: "Hold customer training" and "Improve product list."

24. Move the fourth item from column 1 to the end of column 2.
25. In slide 3 change the layout to "Clip Art & Text," so that the clip art is on the right and the text is on the left; then in the placeholder for the clip art, add the image named "Group Meeting" from the "People" category, which pictures a woman standing with four others sitting. If your copy of PowerPoint doesn't have that clip-art image, use another one of your choice.
26. Create an organization chart in slide 4. Put Norma Lopez, Customer Service, at the top of the chart, with Delbert Green as her assistant on level 2, and three people—Shirley Alvarez, Daniel Truong, and Whitney Sanders, all Customer Representatives—on level 3 below Delbert Green. Hint: To delete an unwanted box on the organization chart, select the box, then press [Backspace].
27. **E** Go to slide 5 and add a square that is about one-fourth the width of the slide. Hint: Use the Rectangle Tool while holding down [Shift]. Add text around the square. Hint: Use the Free Rotate Tool to rotate the text that goes along the left and right sides, but don't rotate the text that goes along the bottom of the square. Type "Quality Products" above the box, "Quick Response" along the right edge (rotated 270 degrees), "Honored Guarantees" along the bottom, and "Regular Follow-up" along the left edge (rotated 90 degrees).
28. **E** Go to slide 6 and double-click on the placeholder labeled "Double click to add graph." Click the down arrow immediately to the right of the Chart Type button to display icons of the various chart types. Click the three-dimensional pie chart (on the fifth row, second column). On the data sheet, change the row labels from "1st Qtr," "2nd Qtr," and so forth, to "Extremely satisfied," "Very Satisfied," "Satisfied," and "Unsatisfied." Hint: You may have to change the width of the columns for these labels to fit. To increase or decrease the width of a column, drag the black line located between the gray column buttons along the top of the data sheet to the left or the right. Beneath those labels type the following numbers into cells A1 through D1: 0.31, 0.42, 0.25, and 0.2, respectively. They indicate the percent of costumers in each category. Close the data sheet and deselect the pie chart.
29. View the entire presentation in Slide Show view.
30. Save your changes.
31. Print a copy of the slides of the presentation. Print them using the Black & White option if you don't have a color printer.
32. Close the file.

Case Problems

1. Data Doctor

Enoch Norbert owns a computer-data-backup service in Framingham, MA. His company, Data Doctor, helps small businesses in the greater Boston area back up their disks and recover damaged data. Enoch wants to use PowerPoint to create a presentation for potential customers.

Open the file P3DATA.PPT, save it to your Student Disk as S3DATA.PPT, and then do the following:

1. To slide 1, add the picture P3DATA.BMP. Adjust the position and alignment of the text and the position of the picture to make the slide attractive and readable.
2. In slide 2, change the layout to Text & Clip Art, then add the PowerPoint clip art "Computer Choking Operator" from the Cartoons category.
3. In slide 3, add the PowerPoint clip art "Duck Smashing PC" from the Cartoons category.
4. In slide 4, add to the center of the slide (below the title) the clip art "Man at Computers" from the People category.
5. Also in slide 4, add a text box with the text "Data Doctor." Position the text box in the middle of the clip art across the two computers.
6. Change the slide layout of slide 5 to Clip Art & Text, then add the clip art "Woman at Computer" from the People category.
7. **E** Change the layout of slide 6 to Graph & Text. In the graph area, create a graph that compares Restore costs (from backed-up data) and Re-enter costs after losing data. In the data sheet, make the titles of four columns the following: "1 hr," "8 hrs," "20 hrs," and "40 hrs" (the restoration times in hours). Make the titles of two rows "Off-site" and "On-site." Delete any other rows. In the "Off-site" row (cells A1 through D1) type the costs (in dollars) for restoring from an off-site backup: 3, 24, 60, 120. In the "On-site" row (cells A2 through D2) type the cost (in dollars) for restoring from an on-site backup: 10, 80, 200, 400. Add a vertical label to the Z-axis: "Cost in dollars." If the X-axis labels have unattractive wrapping of words, increase the width of the graph. You may then have to change the size of the text box to the right of the graph so the graph doesn't cover up text.
8. **E** In slide 7, increase the size of the font in the main text box (below the title) by selecting the text box and dragging I over all the text and then clicking the increase Font Size button five or six times until the longest line of text just fills the width of the text box.
9. **E** Use Slide Show to view all the slides of the presentation.
10. Save the file, then print the slides of the presentation in Black & White.
11. **E** Close the file.

2. Business Plans Plus

Atu Hemuli helps minority entrepreneurs get funding by preparing business plans for them or by editing their existing plans. Atu wants to create a seminar presentation for other professionals who are interested in becoming business-plan consultants.

Open P3BPLAN.PPT, save it to your Student Disk as S3BPLAN.PPT and do the following:

1. To slide 1, add a PowerPoint clip art of "Woman with Binder—Close-Up View" from the People category. Then rearrange, resize, and move the graphics box and the two text boxes to make the title slide look attractive and readable.
2. Insert a new slide 2 into the presentation. Use the "Bulleted List" slide layout. Make the title read "What does a business plan consultant do?" Then add the following bulleted items to the main text: "Guides clients in writing business plans," "Conducts market research," "Gathers financial information," "Projects growth," and "Projects sales potential."
3. **E** In slide 3, change the layout to Text & Graph. Add a pie chart in the graphic box. Hint: After double-clicking the graph icon, click the down arrow to the right of the Chart Type button, and then click pie chart icon (on the fifth row, first column). On the data sheet, change the column labels from "1st Qtr" and "2nd Qtr" to "Formal Business Plan" and "No Business Plan." Delete the labels and information in the other columns. Beneath the column labels, type into cells A1 and B1 the numbers 0.59 and 0.41, respectively. They indicate the percentage in each category. Close the data sheet and deselect the pie chart.
4. **E** In slide 4, add a pie chart similar to the one in slide 3, except the numbers in cells A1 and B1 should be 0.42 and 0.58, respectively.
5. **E** In slide 5, add a pie chart similar to the one in slide 3, except create three column labels: "No planning," "Some planning," and "Formal planning." Then make the label in row one "Planning." Type into cells A1, B1, and C1 the numbers 30, 45, and 25, respectively.
6. Change the layout of slide 6 to Text & Clip Art, then add the clip art "Three People Shaking Hands" from the People category.
7. Change the layout of slide 7 to Text & Clip Art, then add the clip art "Meeting" from the People category.
8. Change the layout of slide 8 to Text & Clip Art, then add the clip art "Man at Podium" from the People category.
9. Use Slide Show to review the entire presentation.
10. Save the file, then print the slides in Black & White.
11. Close the file.

3. Porter and Cole Ad Agency

Sheri Porter and Sherone Cole have combined their talents to found the Porter and Cole Ad Agency. The partners decide that Sheri should prepare a presentation giving the hourly rates for Porter and Cole services and providing a graph on the cost of preparing a document as a function of the number of pages.

Open P3ADAGE.PPT, save it as S3ADAGE, and do the following:

1. In slide 1, increase the font size of the slide title by selecting the text box and double-clicking the Increase Font Size button.
2. **E** In slide 2, to the right of the main text, without changing the slide layout, add the PowerPoint clip art "Woman with Books" from the People category. Hint: Use the Insert Clip Art button on the Standard toolbar, and then resize and move the graphic image so that it fits neatly to the right of the text.
3. In slide 3, replace the clip-art placeholder with the "Man at Computer" image from the People category.
4. In slides 4 and 5, add a clip-art picture to the right of the main text. From the People category, use "Man on Phone" in slide 4 and "Artist" in slide 5.
5. **E** Add a slide 6 with a "Graph" layout. Create a title with the text "Typical Costs of Preparing a Document." Select the graph type by double-clicking the graph placeholder, then clicking the down arrow to the right of the Chart Type button and clicking the line icon (fourth row, first column). Create a graph with the following information:
   a. Column labels (columns A through I, respectively): 0, 5, 10, 15, 20, 25, 30, 35, 40.
   b. First row data (cells A1 through I1, respectively): 0, 300, 250, 200, 175, 150, 125, 125, 125.
   c. Delete other rows and columns.
   d. Z-axis title (make it vertical orientation): "Cost per page"
   e. X-axis title: "Number of pages"
   f. Delete the legend. Hint: Click it, then press [Del].
6. Use Slide Show to review the entire presentation.
7. Save the file, then print the Slides in Black & White.
8. Close the file.

T U T O R I A L 4

Presenting a Slide Show

O B J E C T I V E S

In this tutorial you will:

- Change the slide color scheme and background shading style
- Add text and graphics to the Slide Master
- Modify the color and character of bullets
- Insert slides from another slide presentation
- Apply transitions and builds to slides
- Use the PowerPoint Viewer
- Annotate slides during a slide show
- Create 35mm slides and overhead transparencies

CASE

Report to Investors A year after receiving venture capital from Commercial Financial Bank of Southern California, Patricia Cuevas needs to present her first annual report on Inca Imports International's progress. She will make two presentations: one to the company's board of directors and one to the company stockholders. Patricia decides she can create one slide show for both audiences, and that she should include slides about Inca Imports' successful marketing campaign.

In this tutorial, you will help Patricia create a title slide, gather previously created slides, and arrange and order the slides to create her slide show.

DESIGN PRINCIPLE WINDOW

Preparing for a Presentation Meeting

- Prepare an agenda, including date, time, and place; topics for discussion; names of speakers (and attendees, if it's a small meeting), materials needed (if any).
- Prepare your own presentation. Request help from others, as necessary, and then follow up.
- Check the physical arrangements, including size of room, chairs, tables, podium, and thermostat setting.
- Check the equipment, including microphone, chalkboard (white board), computer with projection system (if you're giving an on-screen presentation), slide projector, overhead projector, VCR and TV (if you're using video).
- Prepare other items, as needed, including beverages, refreshments, pads, pencils, name cards, handouts, and reference materials.

Planning the Presentation

Before starting PowerPoint, Patricia identifies the purpose of and audience for her presentation.

- **Purpose for the presentation:** To present an overview of the progress that Inca Imports has made during the past year
- **Type of presentation:** General presentation
- **Audience for the presentation:** Inca's board of directors; stockholders of Inca Imports at their annual meeting
- **Audience needs:** To quickly gain an overview of Inca's performance over the past year
- **Location of the presentation:** Small boardroom for the board of directors; large conference room at the meeting site for the stockholders
- **Format:** Oral presentation; electronic slide show for the board of directors; 35mm slide show for the stockholders; slide show consisting of five to seven slides

Opening a Blank Presentation

Because she's going to combine previously created slides with new slides, Patricia will open a blank presentation rather than use the AutoContent Wizard. She begins by opening a blank presentation and creating a title slide.

To open a blank presentation:

1. Launch PowerPoint, and from the PowerPoint startup dialog box, click **Blank Presentation**, then click the **OK button**. The New Slide dialog box appears with the AutoLayout selections.

   TROUBLE? If you've already launched PowerPoint, click the New button on the Standard toolbar, then click Blank Presentation and click the OK button.

2. Make sure the Title Slide layout is selected, and click the **OK button**. The placeholders for a title slide appear on the screen in Slide view.
3. If the presentation window is not maximized, click the **Maximize button** of the presentation window. See Figure 4-1.

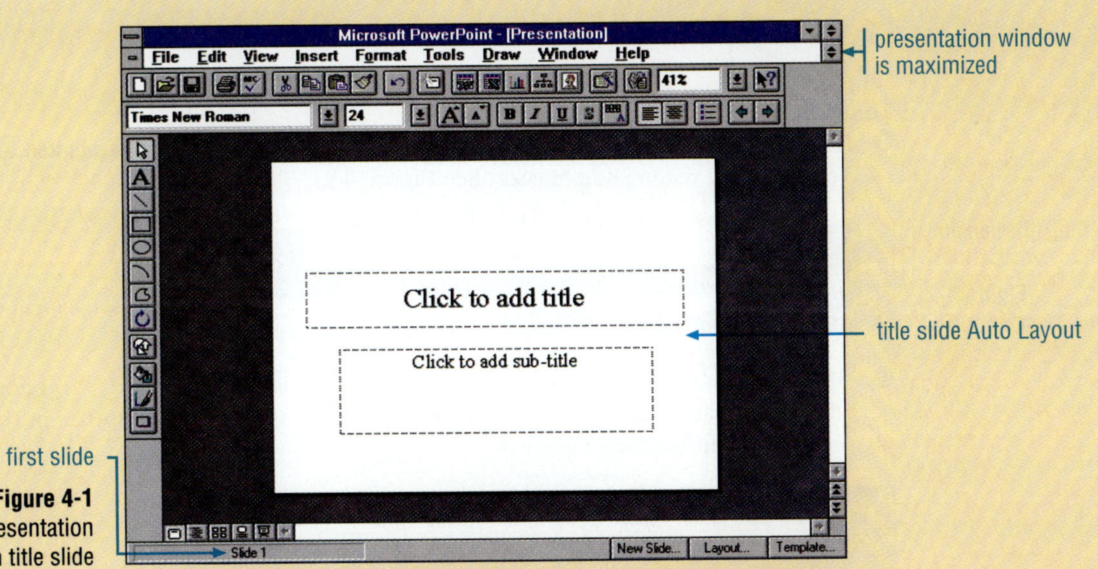

Figure 4-1
Blank presentation with title slide

4. Click the title placeholder and type **Annual Report**.
5. Click the subtitle placeholder and type **Inca Imports International**.
6. Click anywhere outside of any text boxes to deselect them.

Patricia has now created the title slide of the annual report.

Using the Slide Master

When you open a new blank presentation, the default background is white with no design. Patricia wants to select a **color scheme**, that is, an overall color design for the slides in her presentation. When you create a blank presentation, you should choose either a template or a color scheme. Patricia will apply the color scheme to the Slide Master. The **Slide Master** is a slide that contains text and graphics that appear on all of the slides in the presentation and controls the format and color of the text and background on all slides. When you make a change on the master, the change is reflected on all of the slides in the presentation. You can also create a Master for outlines, handouts, and notes.

REFERENCE WINDOW

Modifying a Master

- To display the Master you want, hold down [Shift], then click the appropriate view button. Or you can click View, click Master, then click the desired Master.
- Make changes in color scheme, fonts, bullets, alignment, or in any other formatting feature. Add any desired text, picture, clip art, or other object.
- After modifying the Master, return to another view, such as Slide view or Slide Sorter view by clicking the appropriate view button.

Let's display the Slide Master.

To display the Slide Master:

1. Hold down **[Shift]** and position the mouse arrow over the **Slide View button**. The ToolTip now reads Slide Master. See Figure 4-2.

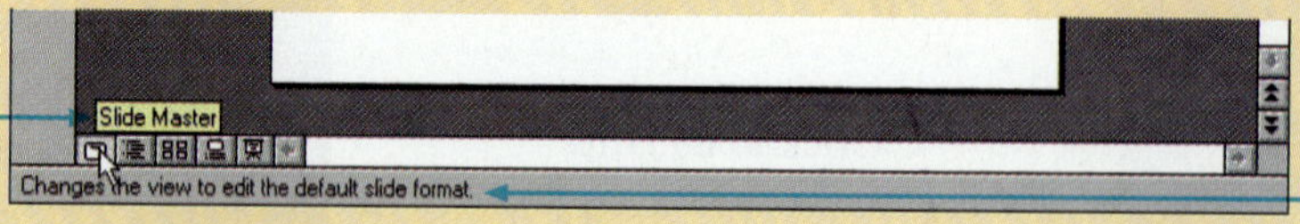

Figure 4-2
Slide Master ToolTip

2. With **[Shift]** still pressed, click the **Slide View button**. Alternatively, you could click **View**, click **Master**, and then click **Slide Master**. The Slide Master appears in the presentation window. See Figure 4-3.

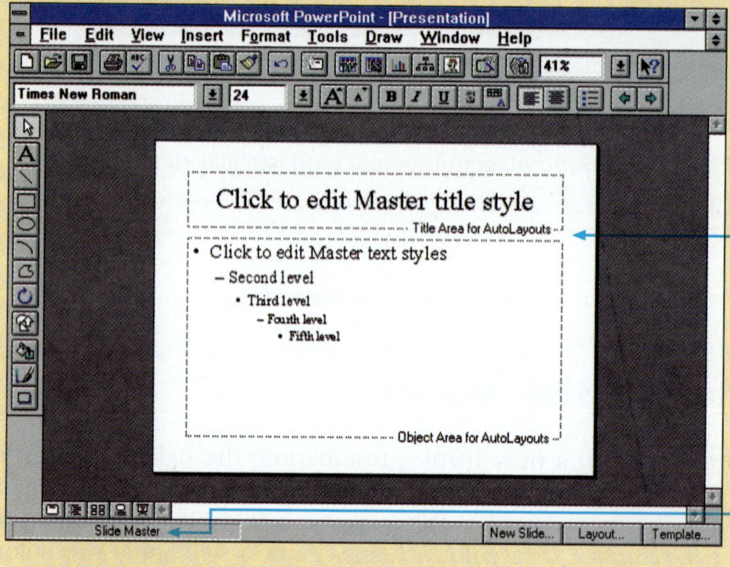

Figure 4-3
Slide Master

Any color scheme you apply or any text or graphics that you add to this slide will appear on all the slides in the presentation.

With the Slide Master in the PowerPoint presentation window, Patricia is now ready to change the color scheme.

Changing the Slide Color Scheme

Patricia knows she could make changes to individual slides without using the Slide Master, but she also knows that certain changes—like adding text, changing the style of bullets, or inserting a logo—should be made on the Slide Master to take effect on all the slides and promote overall consistency in the presentation. Let's change the color scheme of the slides now.

To change the slide color scheme:

❶ Click **Format**, then click **Slide Color Scheme**. The Slide Color Scheme dialog box appears on the screen. See Figure 4-4.

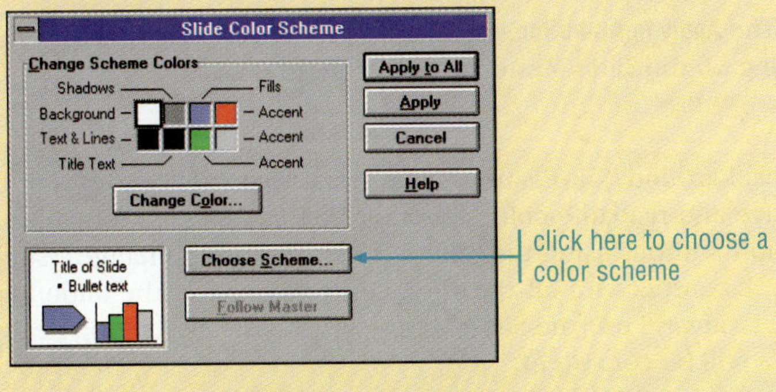

Figure 4-4
Slide Color Scheme dialog box

❷ Click the **Choose Scheme button**. The Choose Scheme dialog box appears. See Figure 4-5. Patricia wants to select a conservative background color for her slides because her audience has a business background.

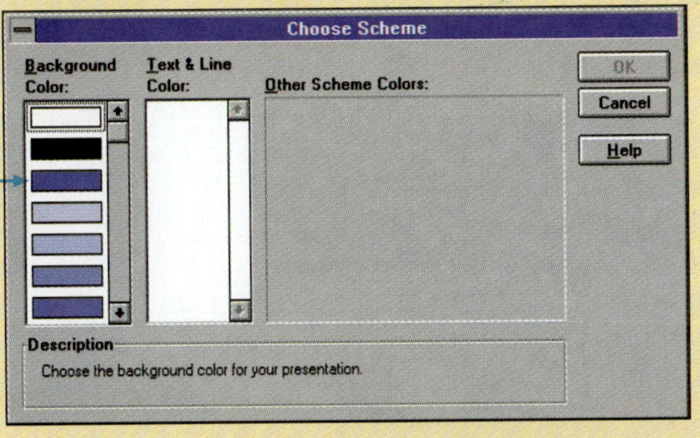

Figure 4-5
Choose Scheme dialog box

❸ Click the first blue tile in the Background Color box of the Choose Scheme dialog box, as shown in Figure 4-5. Now let's pick a white text and line color.

❹ Click the white tile in the Text & Line Color box. PowerPoint now displays some preset color schemes in the Other Scheme Colors box on the Choose Scheme dialog box. See Figure 4-6. With the blue background and white text selected, you can choose variations on that color scheme.

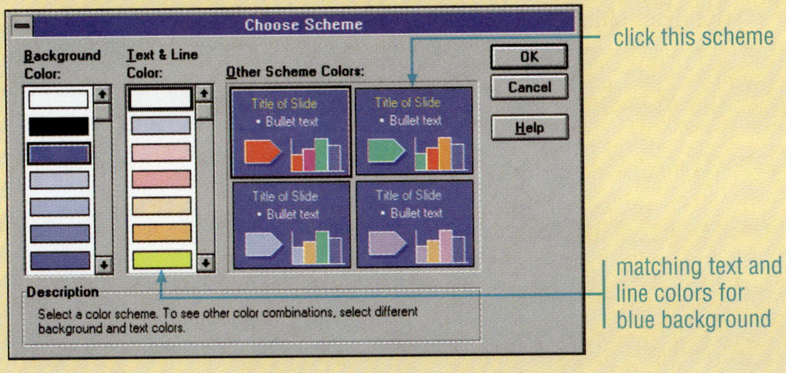

Figure 4-6
Other Scheme Colors box of the Choose Scheme dialog box

5. Click the upper-right tile in the Other Scheme Colors box, as indicated in Figure 4-6, then click the **OK button**. This color scheme keeps the blue background with white letters for the main text as you selected in Steps 3 and 4, but selects yellow as the color for the title on each slide.
6. Click the **Apply to All button**. You could also click the Apply button; because you are working on the Slide Master, any change to this slide will apply to all slides.

The background color is now blue, the title text is yellow, and the main text is white, an attractive and readable color scheme. You can change the color scheme for the entire presentation without using the Slide Master, but other changes, such as modifying bullets and fonts, take effect on all the slides only if you use the Slide Master. Therefore, it's a good idea to always use the Slide Master when you are making design decisions so that all your slides will be consistent.

Although she likes the background color, Patricia decides to change the background from solid blue to a shaded blue. Let's make this change now.

To change the background color to a shade style:

1. Click **Format**, then click **Slide Background**. The Slide Background dialog box appears on the screen. See Figure 4-7.

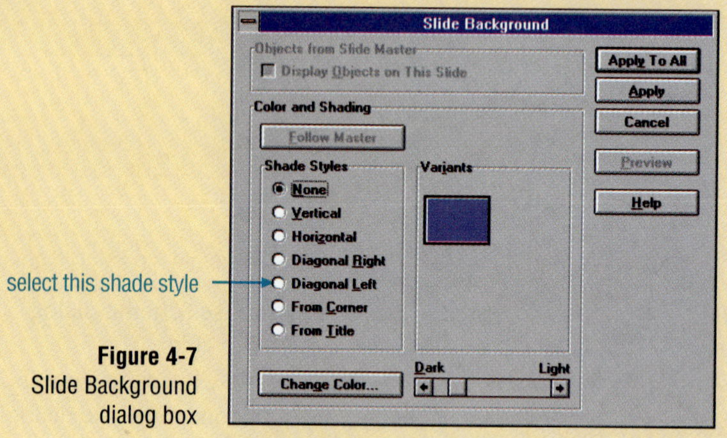

Figure 4-7 Slide Background dialog box

2. In the **Shade Styles box** of the dialog box, click the **Diagonal Left button**; then in the **Variants box**, click the variant that is to the lower right, the style that is lighter along the diagonal and darker in the upper-right and lower-left corners. See Figure 4-8.

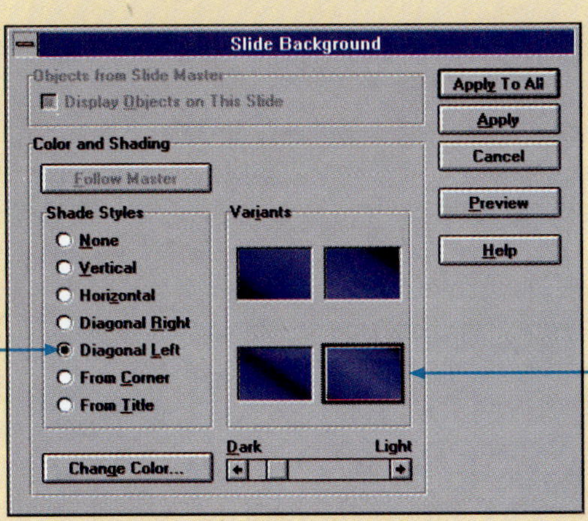

Figure 4-8
Shade Style Variants

❸ Click the **Apply button** or the **Apply to All button**. The new shade style appears on the Slide Master.

You can also change the background color from the Slide Background dialog box. However, by using a preset color scheme from the Slide Color Scheme dialog box, you will always get readable background and font colors in your presentations.

Modifying the Bullets and Font on the Slide Master

Patricia likes the color scheme she has chosen, except that she would like the bullets to be a different color than the main text. She also wants to change the character, or style, used for the bullets. To change the bullets for all the slides in the presentation, she again modifies the Slide Master.

REFERENCE WINDOW

Changing the Bullets

- If you want the change in bullets to affect all slides in the presentation, display the Slide Master by holding down [Shift] and then clicking Slide View. Or click View, click Master, then click Slide Master.
- Click anywhere within the text of the bulleted item.
- Click Format, then click Bullet to display the Bullet dialog box.
- To change the font (so you can select a new bullet character), select a font using the Bullets From list, and then click the desired character.
- To change the color, use the Special Color palette and click the desired color tile.
- Click the OK button.

Let's first change the bullet character and color.

To change the character and color of the bullets:

❶ With the Slide Master still in the presentation window, click anywhere in the phrase "Click to edit Master text styles." Now you're ready to change the bullet style and color.

❷ Click **Format**, then click **Bullet** to display the Bullet dialog box. See Figure 4-9. The current selection of symbols appears in the grid in the middle of the dialog box.

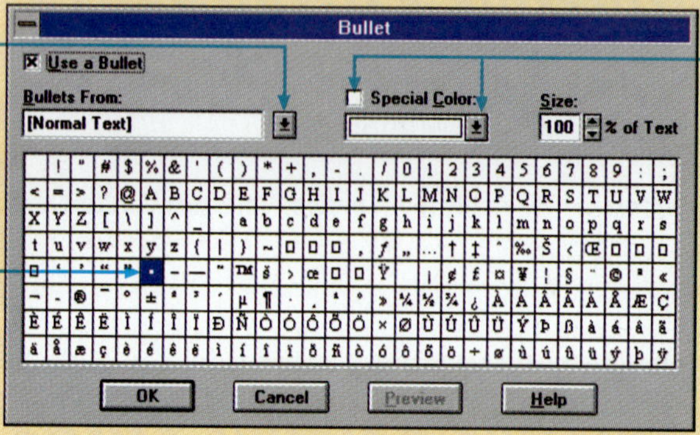

Figure 4-9
Bullet dialog box

❸ Click the **Down arrow button** next to the Bullets From box, then scroll down and click **Wingdings** or some other font that contains a variety of symbols.

TROUBLE? If your Windows system doesn't have a list of fonts available in the Bullets From list, skip Steps 3 and 4 and continue with Step 5, leaving the current bullet symbol as it is.

❹ Click the symbol for a small diamond or for some other symbol that appears in your font. For this presentation, select a simple bullet, like a diamond, square, or circle, that is appropriate for a presentation to stockholders rather than an informal bullet, like a smiley face or a pointing hand. When you click the shapes, the size of the selected shape doubles so you can see it more clearly.

Next, let's change the bullet color.

❺ Click the **Special Color checkbox**. This tells PowerPoint that you want the bullets in your presentation to be a different color from the text color.

❻ Click the **Down arrow button** next to the Special Color box to open the Special Color palette, and click the yellow tile. You have now selected a new bullet character and color. See Figure 4-10.

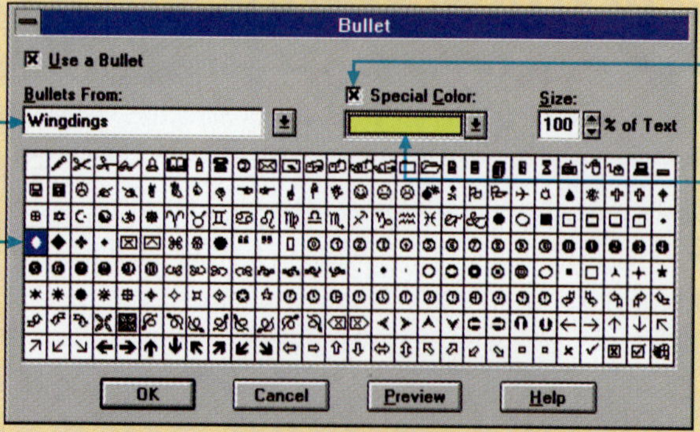

Figure 4-10
Bullet dialog box with new bullet

❼ Click the **OK button** on the Bullet dialog box. The dialog box closes, and the first bulleted item on the Slide Master is a yellow diamond (or whatever shape you chose.)

Having changed the color and style of the bullet, Patricia decides to change the font of the title on the Slide Master to Arial. Let's make that change now.

To change the title font:

1. Click the text box labeled "Click to edit Master title style."
2. Click the **Down arrow button** next to the font box on the Formatting toolbar, then click **Arial**.

   TROUBLE? If your computer system doesn't have Arial, then use another font.

Adding Text to the Slide Master

In addition to changing colors, fonts, and bullets, you can also add text to the Slide Master. The new text will appear on all the slides in the presentation. Patricia wants every slide to contain the company name, so she adds it to the Slide Master.

To add text to the Slide Master:

1. Click the **Text Tool button** on the Drawing Toolbar.
2. Click ↓ just below the lower-left corner of the Object Area for AutoLayout box in the Slide Master.
3. Change the Font to **Arial** and the Font Size to **20 point**.
4. Type **Inca Imports International** and then click anywhere outside the slide to deselect the text box. The Slide Master now includes the company name. See Figure 4-11.

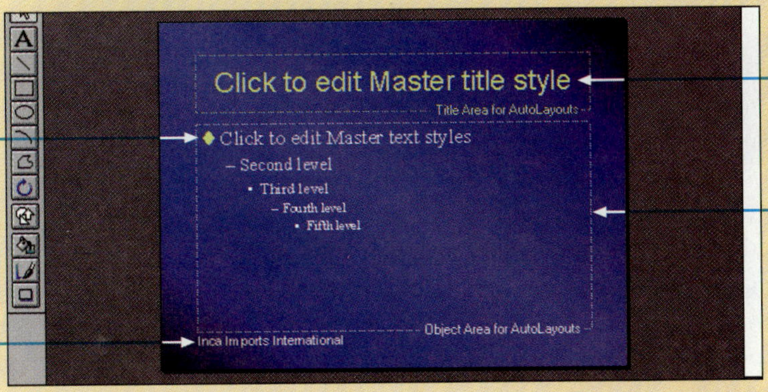

Figure 4-11 Slide Master with company name

TROUBLE? If the position of the company name isn't similar to what you see in Figure 4-11, move the "Inca Imports International" text box to the desired location.

If Patricia had chosen a template, the color scheme, background, font, font style, and font sizes would have been chosen for her. Instead, she decided to make these decisions herself by using the Slide Master.

Adding a Logo to the Slide Master

Finally, Patricia wants to add the Inca Imports International logo to the Slide Master, so that the logo will appear on every slide in the presentation. To add a picture to the Slide Master, you follow the same procedure as adding a picture to a regular slide.

To add a picture to a Slide Master:

1. Click **Insert**, then click **Picture** to display the Insert Picture dialog box.
2. If it's not there already, insert the Student Disk into drive A or B, then make that disk drive the current drive in the Insert Picture dialog box.
3. Click **iiilogo.bmp** to select the logo, then click the **OK button**. PowerPoint inserts the logo into the middle of the Slide Master. Because the logo will be on all the slides, Patricia wants to make it smaller and move it into the upper-left corner of the slide.
4. Drag the logo on top of the box labeled "Title Area for AutoLayout" so its upper-left corner is located at or near the upper-left corner of the title text box.
5. Drag the lower-right resize handle up and to the left so that the height of the image is the same size as the text box. Your Slide Master window should look like Figure 4-12.

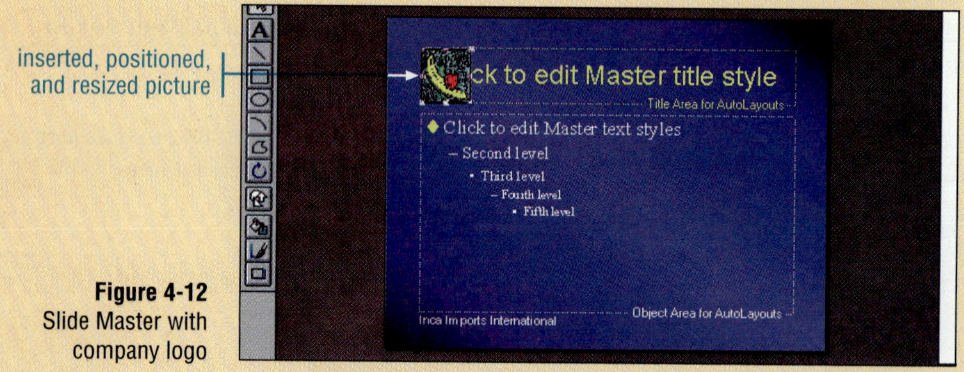

Figure 4-12 Slide Master with company logo

6. Click the **title text box** to the right of the logo to select the title box, then click the edge of the text box to display the resize handles.
7. Drag the lower-left resize handle to the right so that the left edge of the text box is to the right of the logo, and then click the **Left Alignment button** on the Formatting toolbar so that the title is left aligned rather than centered. See Figure 4-13.

This completes Patricia's changes to the Slide Master, as shown in Figure 4-13. Satisfied with the slide design she has created for her presentation, Patricia changes back to Slide view.

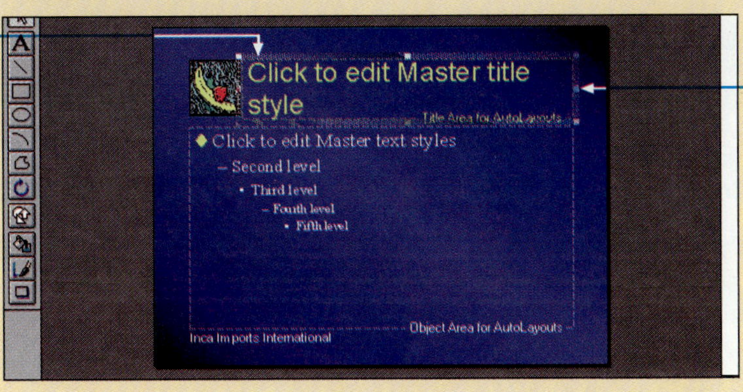

Figure 4-13
Completed Slide Master with reformatted title box

8. Click the **Slide View button** at the bottom of the presentation window to switch back to Slide view. As you can see, the title slide is now formatted like the Slide Master.

Patricia has worked for about fifteen minutes, so she decides to save the slide presentation changes to this point.

To save the slide presentation:

1. Click the **Save button** on the Formatting toolbar, then save the presentation to the Student Disk using the filename S4FILE1. The Summary Info dialog box appears on the screen.
2. Leave the title as Annual Report, and then by clicking in each box or pressing **[Tab]** to move to each box, change the Subject to "Report to Board of Directors and Stockholders," the Author to "Patricia Cuevas," the Keywords to "Annual Report to Stockholders," and leave the Comments blank.
3. Click the **OK button**. PowerPoint saves the presentation to the disk.

If you want to take a break and resume the tutorial at a later time, you can do so now. If you exit PowerPoint, launch the program again when you want to resume working, and open the presentation file S4FILE1.PPT. Then continue with the next section.

Inserting Slides from Another Presentation

Patricia Cuevas's first task in this annual report presentation is to review with her audience the products and services offered by Inca Imports. That information, however, already exists in the presentation developed earlier by Enrique Hoffmann for the marketing division. So Patricia decides to insert slides from Enrique's presentation into the current one.

REFERENCE WINDOW

Inserting Slides from an Existing Presentation

- Get into Slide view, then display the slide after which you want to insert the existing presentation slides.
- Click Insert, then click Slides from File.
- Select the disk and filename that contains the existing presentation, then click the OK button.

Let's insert slides from an existing presentation now.

To insert slides from an existing file:

1. With the title slide of the annual report still in the presentation window in Slide view, click **Insert**, then click **Slides from File**. PowerPoint displays the Insert File dialog box.

   When you insert slides from another presentation, you must insert the entire file, then delete the slides you don't want.

2. With the Drives set to the drive containing the Student Disk, click **c4file1.ppt** in the File Name list, and then click the **OK button**. PowerPoint retrieves the existing presentation and displays a message that the slides from the disk are being updated to match the color scheme on the Slide Master of the current presentation.

Slide 2 appears in the presentation window. This is the title slide from the earlier presentation. You can delete this slide.

To delete a slide:

1. Click **Edit**, then click **Delete Slide** to delete the current slide. The new slide 2 is titled "Providing Quality Produce." See Figure 4-14. The slide has the color scheme of the current slide presentation, not of the original presentation from which it came.

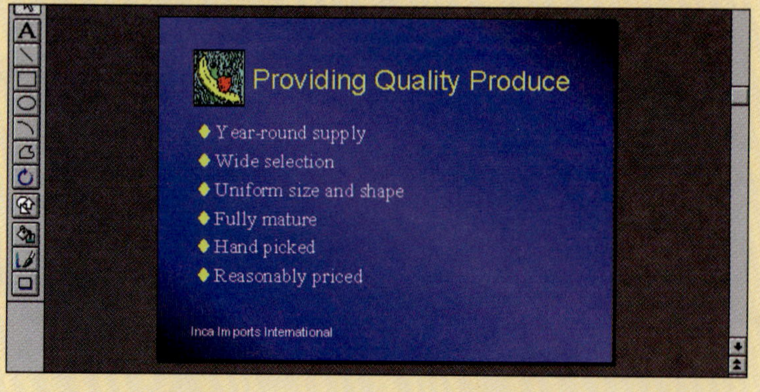

Figure 4-14 New slide 2 with updated design

Patricia now has all the slides she needs from past slide presentations.

Completing the Slide Presentation

Next Patricia needs to change the order of the slides to meet the needs of this presentation, delete unwanted slides, and add new slides as needed. To sort the slides, you'll use Slide Sorter view. You can also change the order of slides in Outline view. Let's sort the slides now.

To change the order of the slides:

❶ Click the **Slide Sorter View button** at the bottom of the presentation window. PowerPoint displays the slides of the presentation and the Slide Sorter toolbar appears below the Standard toolbar. Patricia wants to move slide 3, "Meeting Your Needs," so it becomes slide 2.

❷ Drag slide 3 to the left, and watch as a vertical line follows the pointer. Release the mouse button when the vertical line is between slides 1 and 2. Patricia decides to delete slide 4, "Reducing Time to Market."

❸ Click **slide 4** to make it the current slide, then press **[Del]** or click **Edit**, then click **Delete Slide**. PowerPoint deletes the slide from the presentation. See Figure 4-15.

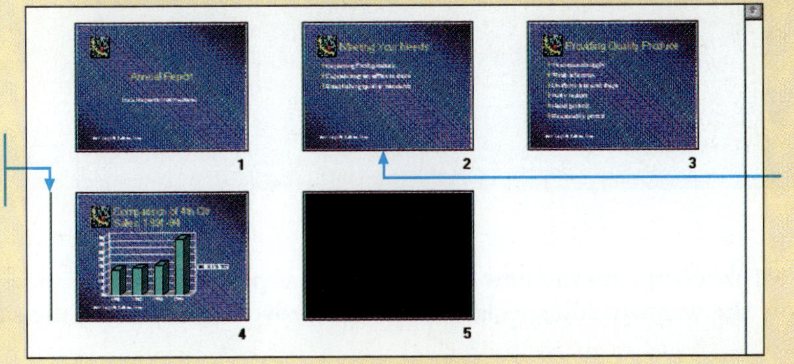

Figure 4-15
Slide Sorter view after moving a slide and deleting a slide

Next, Patricia wants to change the wording in the title of slide 2. You can't change text from within Slide Sorter view. You must be in Slide view or Outline view to edit slide text. Let's change the title of the slide now.

To edit slide text:

❶ Click **slide 2**, then click the **Slide View button** at the bottom of the presentation window. PowerPoint displays slide 2 in the presentation window.

❷ Using methods you've learned previously, change the title from "Meeting Your Needs" to "Meeting Customer Needs." Then deselect the title text box.

Now Patricia wants to add a slide to the presentation that summarizes the performance of her company.

To add new slides:

1. From within Slide view, move to slide 4 of the presentation.
2. Click the **Insert New Slide button** on the Standard toolbar to insert a new slide into the presentation. PowerPoint displays the New Slide dialog box. You could also have clicked the New Slide button at the bottom of the presentation window.
3. Click the layout titled "Bulleted list," the second slide in the first row, then click the **OK button**.
4. Click the title placeholder and type **Inca's Solid Performance**.
5. Click the main text (bulleted list) text box and type three bulleted items: **Improved products and services**, **Implemented new marketing plan**, and **Increased profitability**.
6. Click outside the text boxes to see the completed slide. See Figure 4-16.

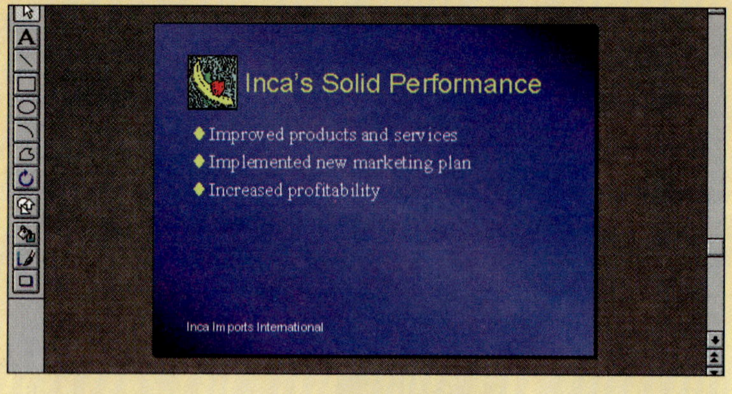

Figure 4-16
Completed new slide

That completes the new slide 5. Patricia is pleased with the slides in her presentation. Now she wants to add special effects to improve the interest of the slide show.

Adding Transition Effects

The first special effect that Patricia wants to add is called a transition. A **transition** is a method of moving one slide off the screen and bringing another slide onto the screen during a slide show. You must be in Slide Sorter view to add transitions.

REFERENCE WINDOW

Adding Transition Effects

- Get into Slide Sorter view and select the slide or slides to which you want to add a transition effect.
- Click the Down arrow button in the Transition Effects box on the Formatting toolbar to display a list of transition effects.
- Click the desired transition effect.

Let's add a transition to all of the slides in the presentation.

To add a transition effect:

❶ Click the **Slide Sorter View button** at the bottom of the presentation window to change to Slide Sorter view.

❷ Click **Edit**, then click **Select All** to select all the slides in the presentation. Now when you apply a slide transition, all the slides will have that transition. Currently, the Formatting toolbar shows "No Transition" in the Transition Effects box. See Figure 4-17.

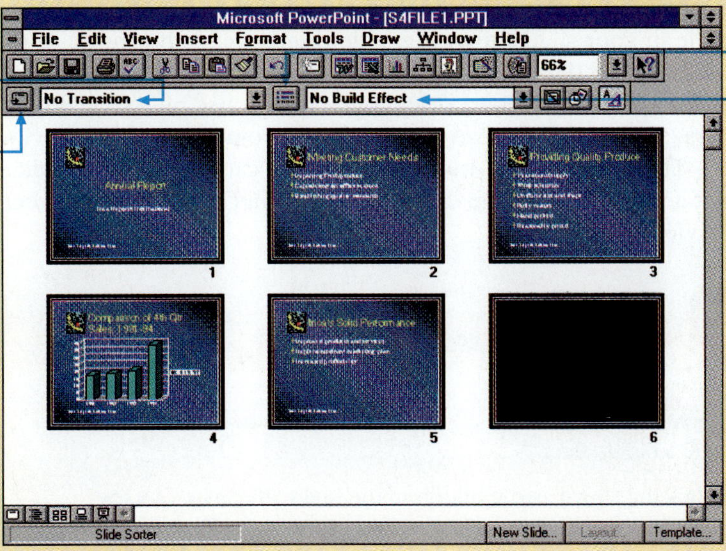

Figure 4-17
All six slides selected

❸ Click the **Down arrow button** in the Transition Effects box in the Slide Sorter toolbar to display the list of transitions.

❹ Scroll through the list until **Dissolve** appears, then click that method of transition. If you watched carefully, you saw PowerPoint demonstrate the dissolve transition with the first slide.

❺ Click anywhere outside of a slide to deselect the slides. PowerPoint has placed a transition icon below the lower-left corner of each slide. See Figure 4-18.

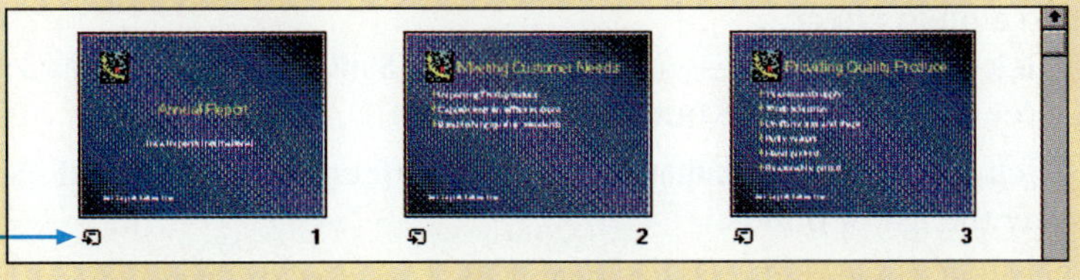

Figure 4-18
Transition icons in Slide Sorter view

You can test the transition of any slide now by clicking on the transition icon. Let's try it.

❻ Click the transition icon below slide 4. As you can see, PowerPoint momentarily displays slide 3 at that location, then performs the transition to slide 4. Click any of the transition icons to see how the transition looks for that slide.

You have now added transitions to the slides. You added the same transition to all six slides, but if you wanted, you could have selected only one slide and created a unique transition for only that slide.

Adding Build Effects

Having added transitions to the slides, Patricia is ready to add another special effect: builds. A **build** (also known as a **progressive disclosure**) is a feature that allows you to progressively display individual bulleted items, one item at a time. For example, if a slide has several bulleted items, you can add a build to the slide so that when you first display the slide in your slide show, the slide title appears, but none of the bulleted items. Then when you press [Spacebar] or click the left mouse button, the first bulleted item appears. When you press [Spacebar] or click the left mouse button again, the second bulleted item appears, and so on. You can also tell PowerPoint to dim the previous item as a new one is added. The advantage of builds is that you can focus your audience's attention on one item at a time, without the distractions of other items on the screen. You must be in Slide Sorter view to add builds.

REFERENCE WINDOW

Adding a Build Effect

- In Slide Sorter view, select the slide or slides to which you want to add a build effect.
- Click the Down arrow button in the Build Effects box on the Formatting toolbar to display a list of transition effects.
- Click the desired build effect.
- To dim previous points in the build, click the Build button to the left of the Build Effects box to display the Build dialog box, select a dim color, and then click the OK button.

Let's add a build effect now.

To add a build effect:

1. Click **slide 2**, then press and hold down **[Shift]**, and click **slides 3** and **5** to select the three slides that have bulleted lists.
2. Click the **Down arrow button** in the Build Effects box in the Slide Sorter toolbar to display the list of builds.
3. Scroll down and click **Wipe Right**. This specifies the type of build effect you want. In this case, the text in each bulleted item appears on the screen from left to right as if someone wiped it onto the screen. Now Patricia wants PowerPoint to dim the old bulleted item, while displaying a new one. This is called "dimming previous points."
4. Click the **Build button** on the Slide Sorter toolbar. PowerPoint displays the Build dialog box.
5. Click the **Dim Previous Points check box**. Below the Dim Previous Points checkbox is a colored bar that represents the color of the dimmed item. Let's change that color to blue-green.

6. Click the **Down arrow button** to the right of the dim-color bar and click the **blue-green (cyan) color tile**. See Figure 4-19.

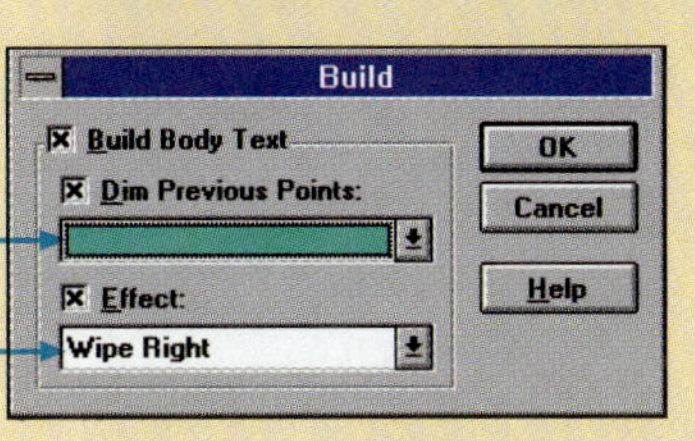

Figure 4-19
Build dialog box

7. Click the **OK button**. PowerPoint adds build effect icons below slides 2, 3, and 5, the three slides to which you have added build effects. See Figure 4-20.

Figure 4-20
Slide with build effect icons

8. Click anywhere outside the slides to deselect them.
   You have now added build effects to the appropriate slides. You could have added different build effects to each slide by selecting each slide individually and then completing Steps 2 through 7 above.

You can't see a build while in Slide Sorter view; you must be in Slide Show view. Let's run the completed slide show to view our special effects—the transitions and builds.

Running the Slide Show

Patricia has completed her slide show, and she's now ready to view it. Let's view the presentation using the Slide Show view.

To view the completed presentation:

1. Click **slide 1** in Slide Sorter view so that your presentation will begin with slide 1.
2. Click the **Slide Show button** at the bottom of the presentation window to begin the slide presentation. The title slide, "Annual Report," appears on the screen.
3. Press **[Spacebar]** to advance to the next slide. (You can also use the arrow keys, the page up and page down keys, or the mouse button.) Only the title of slide 2 appears on the screen, because this is a build slide, which will disclose the bulleted items one at a time as you go through the slide show.
4. Press **[Spacebar]** to display the first bulleted item under "Meeting Customer Needs."
5. Press **[Spacebar]** to display the second bulleted item and dim the first one. See Figure 4-21.

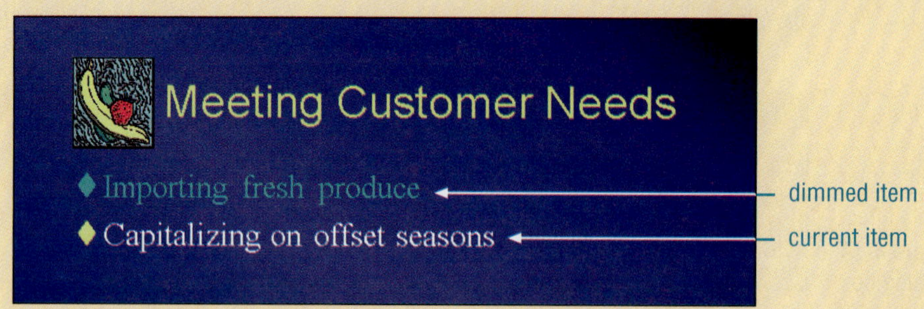

Figure 4-21 Build effect with dimmed previous item

6. Continue through the slide show, pressing **[Spacebar]** to advance from one slide to the next or, within a build slide, from one point to the next. When you get to the last slide, the one with the black background, stop there.

   TROUBLE? If you advanced past the last slide, PowerPoint returned you to the Slide Sorter view. Just click the Slide Show button again, then press [End] to return to the last slide.

   At this point, Patricia decides that she wants to look at the "Inca's Solid Performance" slide again.

7. Click the *right* mouse button. This moves the presentation backwards to the previous slide. Notice that when you go back to the previous slide, all the bulleted items appear and they are in the normal color, not dimmed. If you wanted to return to a previous slide and go backwards through the build effect, you could press [←] multiple times. (This does not work with the right mouse button.)

8. Press **[Esc]** to return to Slide Sorter view.

Patricia is pleased with the results. She saves the final version of her slide show.

To save the slide show:

1. Click the **Save button** on the Standard toolbar to save the presentation file using the filename S4FILE1.PPT.

Annotating Slides During a Slide Show

While Patricia rehearses her slide presentation and during the actual presentation to the stockholders, she will annotate certain slides to draw attention to important points. To **annotate** in PowerPoint means to make temporary freehand marks on the slide during a slide presentation. The annotations are not saved to the disk with the presentation itself.

REFERENCE WINDOW

Annotating a Slide

- While running a slide show in Slide Show view or in the PowerPoint Viewer, advance to the slide you wish to annotate.
- Click the Freehand annotation icon in the lower-right corner of the screen.
- Use the pencil mouse pointer to make temporary marks on the slide.

Let's annotate the presentation now.

To annotate a slide:

1. From Slide Sorter view, click slide 3 to select it.
2. Click the **Slide Show button** . Slide 3 appears in Slide Show view.
3. Press **[Spacebar]** six times to see the last bulleted item, "Reasonably priced."
4. Move the mouse to display the mouse pointer on the screen and to display the Freehand annotation icon in the lower-right corner of the screen. See Figure 4-22.

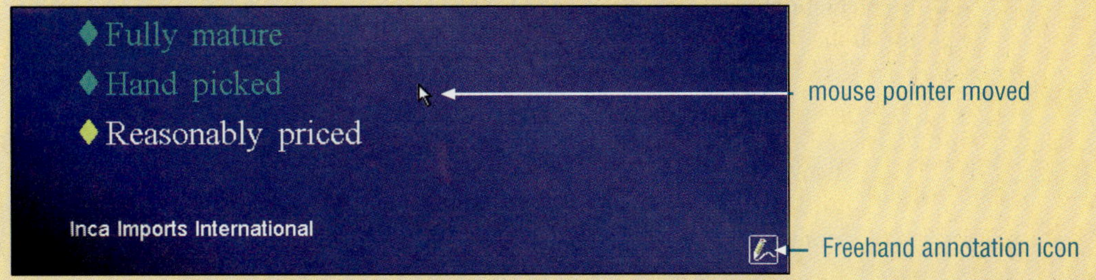

Figure 4-22 Freehand annotation icon

Patricia wants to emphasize that Inca produce is reasonably priced, neither the highest nor the lowest in the industry.

5. Click the **Freehand annotation icon** in the lower-right corner of the screen. The mouse pointer becomes .
6. Position under the "R" in "Reasonably," then hold down the left mouse button while you drag the pointer to underline that word. Then release the mouse button. See Figure 4-23. Patricia rehearses what she will say to emphasize the meaning of "reasonably priced."

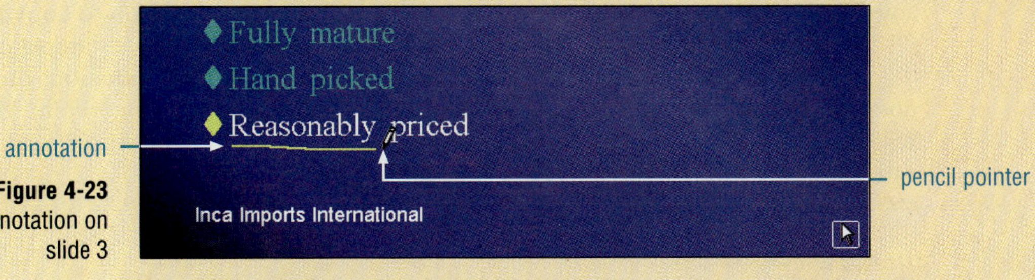

Figure 4-23 Annotation on slide 3

7. Press **[Spacebar]**. The annotations disappear and the next slide appears on the screen.
8. Press **[Esc]** to quit the slide show.
9. Exit PowerPoint.

After rehearsing her presentation several times, Patricia feels confident about making the presentation to the stockholders.

DESIGN PRINCIPLE WINDOW

Tips on Electronic Presentations

- Don't feel that you have to include transitions and builds in your slides. Unnecessary transitions and builds will distract your audience from the message of the presentation.
- If you include transitions, use only one type of transition for all the slides.
- If you include builds, use only one type of build for all the build slides.
- If you are have a tendency to get nervous during a presentation, avoid using the mouse to advance the slides and to make annotations. The audience can see a jittery mouse pointer. Instead, use the [Spacebar] to advance slides.
- Avoid excessive annotations on slides. Annotations can look sloppy if done to excess.

If you want to take a break and resume the tutorial at a later time, you can do so now. When you resume working, make sure the Windows Program Manager is on screen and that your Student Disk with the file S4FILE1.PPT is in the appropriate drive. Then continue with the next section.

■ ■ ■

Using the PowerPoint Viewer

You could run all your presentations from the PowerPoint program, but what if you want to give a presentation on a computer that doesn't have PowerPoint installed? In that case, you could use the PowerPoint Viewer. The **PowerPoint Viewer** is a separate program (shipped by Microsoft on a separate disk) that you can use to show your presentation on any Windows computer. The Microsoft PowerPoint license allow you to copy the Viewer disk and to install the Viewer program on other computers without additional charge.

Patricia wants to get Angelena Cristenas' opinion on her presentation, but Angelena doesn't have PowerPoint on her computer. Patricia brings the PowerPoint Viewer disk with her and runs her presentation from that. Let's first install the Viewer program. You can use your own or someone else's computer.

To install PowerPoint Viewer:

1. Make sure you have a copy of the PowerPoint Viewer disk, which is Disk 11 in the PowerPoint 4.0 package.

   TROUBLE? You might not be allowed to install Viewer on a computer in a lab or on a network. If you don't have the PowerPoint Viewer disk, consult your instructor or technical support person. If they can't provide you with a disk and you don't have your own PowerPoint package, skip this section. Similarly, if PowerPoint Viewer is already installed on your computer, you can skip this section.

2. Launch Windows so that the Program Manager is on the screen.
3. Insert the PowerPoint Viewer disk into a disk drive, click **File**, click **Run**, type **a:vsetup**, and click the **OK button**. Then follow the instructions on your screen to complete the installation.

Patricia is now ready to run her slide presentation using the Viewer.

To use the Viewer:

1. Double-click the **PowerPoint Viewer icon** in the Windows Program Manager. See Figure 4-24. The Microsoft PowerPoint Viewer dialog box appears on the screen.

Figure 4-24
PowerPoint Viewer icon

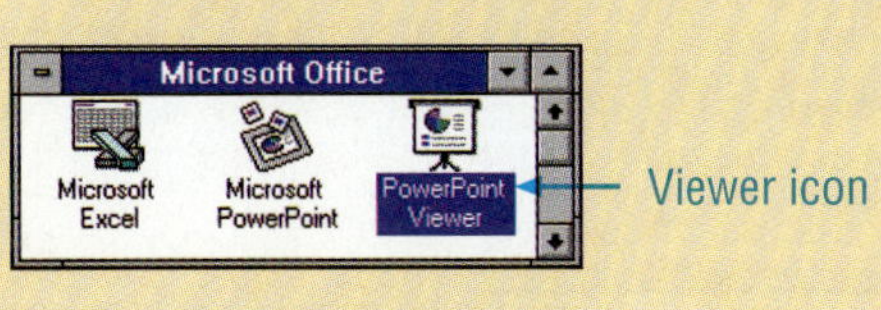

2. From the Microsoft PowerPoint Viewer dialog box, select the disk drive that contains your Student Disk, then select **s4file1.ppt**, and click the **Show button**. Clicking the Show button in the PowerPoint Viewer dialog box is the same as clicking the Slide Show button in the presentation window.
3. Press **[Spacebar]** or click the left mouse button to run through the presentation. Feel free to press **[Esc]** to stop the slide show whenever you want. When you finish, you will be returned to the PowerPoint Viewer dialog box.
4. Click the **Quit button** to return to the Windows Program Manager.

Angelena liked Patricia's presentation.

Preparing 35mm Slides

Patricia will present the electronic slide show to the board of directors in a suitably equipped conference room at Inca Imports. The conference room at the stockholders meeting, however, does not have the equipment necessary to run an electronic slide show, so Patricia plans to use 35mm slides. Because the presentation to the stockholders is very important, Patricia also makes black-and-white transparency masters as a back-up to the slides.

Inca Imports International, like most small businesses, lacks the facilities to make 35mm slides or print color output from computer files, but all large U.S. cities have service bureaus that can convert computer files into 35mm slides, provided the files are in the correct format, usually PostScript. You should contact a service bureau near you for details. Check the yellow pages of your telephone book under "Typesetting."

PowerPoint also supports the services of Genigraphics Corporation, a service bureau that handles 35mm slides, color overheads, and posters. With headquarters in Memphis, Tennessee, Genigraphics has facilities in fourteen major cities around the United States. The PowerPoint disks contain the software necessary to prepare and deliver slides to Genigraphics. Patricia therefore decides to use Genigraphics to prepare her slides.

Note: In the following procedure, you will prepare the presentation as if you were going to pay for commercial slide preparation, but you won't actually send the presentation file to Genigraphics.

To prepare 35mm slides in Genigraphics format:

1. Launch PowerPoint again, and open S4FILE1.PPT.
2. Click **File**, then click **Slide Setup**. PowerPoint displays the Slide Setup dialog box. See Figure 4-25.

Go through steps - don't send out

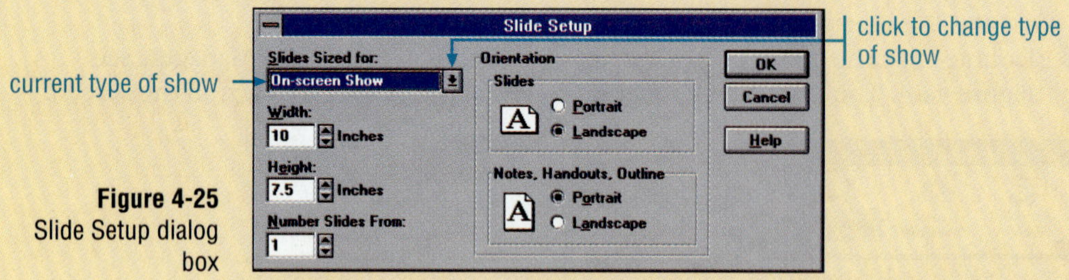

Figure 4-25
Slide Setup dialog box

❸ Click the **Down arrow button** next to "Slide Sized for," and select **35mm Slides**. PowerPoint adjusts the width and height of each slide so it is proportioned for 35mm slides. Click the **OK button**.

Now you will output the presentation to a disk file in the Genigraphics format.

❹ Click **File**, click **Print** to display the Print dialog box, then click the **Printer button** to display the Print Setup dialog box.

Here you will select the printer driver for Genigraphics. A **printer driver** is a disk file that provides information about a printer so that your applications software can prepare output for that printer. Some printer drivers, like the one for Genigraphics, don't actually send the file to a printer but rather create a disk file in a special format. The Genigraphics driver also displays dialog boxes to get additional information when you "print" your presentation to disk.

❺ Click **Genigraphics Driver on GENI:**, then click the **OK button**. PowerPoint returns to the Print dialog box. Most of the options in the dialog box are dimmed because the Genigraphics printer driver contains its own set of options.

TROUBLE? The Genigraphics Driver will only be listed if your computer has the complete PowerPoint installation. If you don't see the driver, see your instructor or technical support person.

You are now prepared to "print" the presentation in Genigraphics format—that is, send the presentation to a disk file. Let's do that now.

To prepare the Genigraphics file:

❶ Make sure the Print What text box contains **Slides (With Builds)**. By selecting Slides (With Builds) you are telling Genigraphics to create a separate slide with each of the progressive disclosure items for the build slides. That means Patricia will end up with eighteen 35mm slides, not just six.

❷ Click the **OK button** on the Print dialog box. The Genigraphics driver displays a dialog box requesting more information. See Figure 4-26. Patricia knows that she can

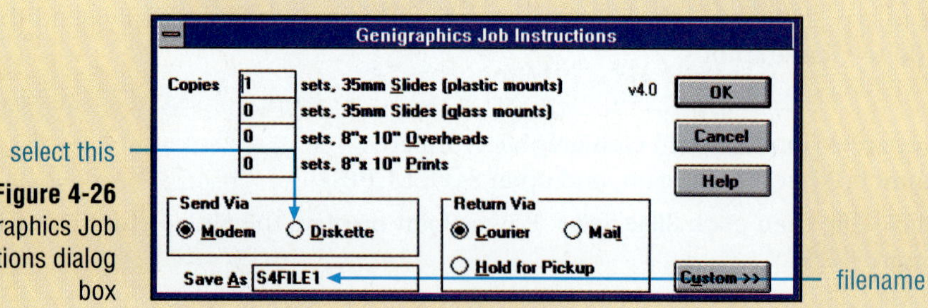

Figure 4-26
Genigraphics Job Instructions dialog box

use her modem to send the file directly to Genigraphics Corporation, or she can save the file on a disk. Patricia decides to save it to a disk, then mail the disk to Genigraphics using an overnight courier service like Federal Express or UPS. You will save the file to your Student Disk.

Notice that at the bottom of the dialog box, the filename in the Save As box is S4FILE1, the file currently in the PowerPoint presentation window.

3. Click **Diskette** in the Send Via box, make sure **Courier** is selected in the Return Via box, and then click the **OK button**. The Genigraphics dialog box closes and the Save As dialog box appears. Notice the default filename is the same as the one that was in the Genigraphics dialog box, and the Genigraphics driver added the file extension.GNA. You can change the filename, but you must leave the Genigraphics extension so their equipment will recognize the file.
4. In the Save As dialog box, change the Drives box to display the disk drive where your Student Disk is located, and click the **OK button**. The file S4FILE1.GNA is saved to the disk. Next the Genigraphics driver displays the Genigraphics Billing Information dialog box.
5. Fill out the information in the dialog box with your name, address, phone number, and so forth. Click the **COD button** so you don't have to fill in a credit card number. Then click the **OK button**. You'll see a message telling you that a file with 18 slides has been saved and that you should send the file to Genigraphics for processing.
6. After reading the message, click the **OK button**.

Patricia has now prepared the file S4FILE1.GNA to send to Genigraphics.

Preparing Overheads

Patricia's presentation to the stockholders is very important, so she decides to be on the safe side and create black and white overheads of the presentation in case the slide projector doesn't work. With PowerPoint, you can prepare overhead transparency masters quickly and easily. You simply have to change the slide design to overheads. In general, designs that work well for slides might not work as well for black-and-white overheads. PowerPoint provides several templates for black-and-white overheads. Patricia decides to change the slide design to one specifically created for black-and-white overheads. She could do this by choosing a new template or by using the Pick a Look Wizard. You already know how to choose a new template, so let's use the Pick a Look Wizard to change the design to overheads.

To change the design to overheads:

1. Click the **Pick a Look Wizard button** on the Standard toolbar. PowerPoint displays the Step 1 dialog box of the Pick a Look Wizard.
2. Read the information on the dialog box, then click the **Next button** to proceed to Step 2. See Figure 4-27. Here the Wizard asks you which type of output you want.

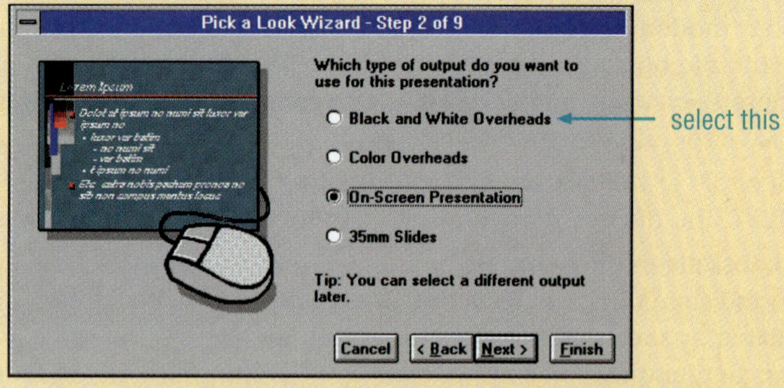

Figure 4-27
Step 2 of Pick a Look Wizard

3. Click **Black and White Overheads**, then click the **Next button**. You can also create color overheads, but that requires a color printer. Step 3 of the Wizard now appears on the screen, where you will select a template design. Only templates specifically designed for black-and-white overheads appear in the list.
4. Click **Double Lines**, a template design with a shaded line across the overhead, then click the **Next button**. PowerPoint displays step 4 of the Wizard. Here Patricia selects the type of material that she wants in her slide presentation. She decides she wants only full-page slides (overheads).
5. Make sure the **Full-Page Slides checkbox** is selected and the other three options are deselected. Then click the **Next button**. Now the Wizard displays the Slide Options. Patricia doesn't want any of these slide options.
6. Make sure none of the slide options is selected, then click the **Next button**. You can now see the final dialog box of the Pick a Look Wizard.
7. Click the **Finish button**. PowerPoint updates the color scheme of the slides. The black-and-white overheads appear in the presentation window.

Patricia observes that when the Pick a Look Wizard added the Double Lines template, it removed the Inca Imports logo from the Slide Master. She decides to add the logo back to the Slide Master. Patricia also realizes that with overheads, you don't need a slide to mark the end of the presentation, so she deletes the final blank slide from the overhead masters. She will then save the overhead presentation file and print the overheads.

To complete the overhead presentation:

1. From slide sorter view, click slide 6, and press **[Del]**. This slide is deleted from the presentation.
2. Add the Inca Imports logo from the file IIILOGO.BMP to the Slide Master in the same position you had it in before, then return to Slide Sorter view. (If you need help, refer back to the section "Adding a Logo to the Slide Master.") See Figure 4-28. The logo appears in color on the screen but will be black and white when you print the overhead masters.

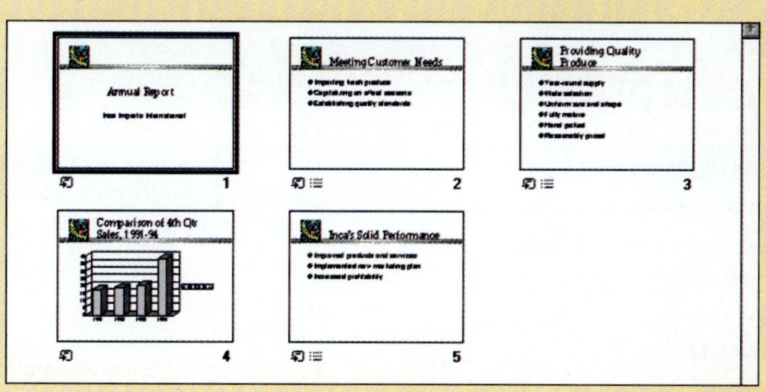

Figure 4-28
Overheads after adding logo

Now Patricia wants to save the overhead presentation using a different filename. She also wants to change the orientation of the printing from landscape, which is wider than it is tall, to portrait, which is taller than it is wide. Overheads fit the projector better if they are in portrait view.

❸ Click **File**, click **Slide Setup** to display the Slide Setup dialog box, click **Portrait** in the Slides orientation box, then click the **OK button**. The page orientation now appears in portrait view. See Figure 4-29.

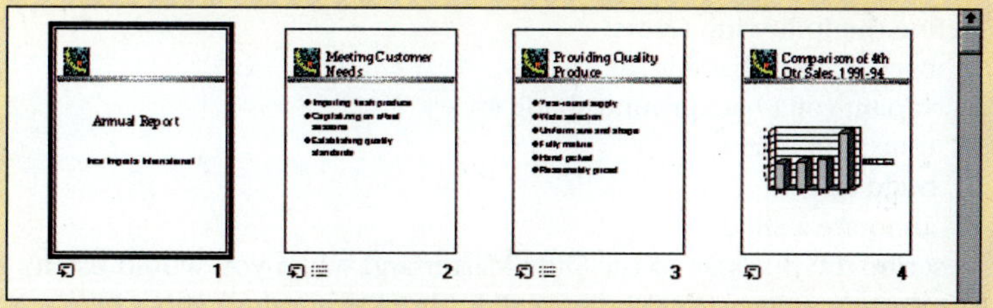

Figure 4-29
Overheads in portrait orientation

❹ Click **File**, click **Save As**, and then save the presentation to your Student Disk using the filename S4FILE2.PPT. You will use the same Summary Info as you did earlier, so just click the **OK button**. Patricia now prints the overheads.

❺ Click **File**, then click **Print**. PowerPoint displays the Print dialog box. The current printer is listed as Genigraphics Driver on GENI. You'll have to change back to your normal printer.

❻ Click the **Printer button** to display the Printer Setup dialog box, click the name of your printer in the Printers box, and then click the **OK button**. PowerPoint returns to the Print dialog box.

❼ Make sure that **Slides (without builds)** is selected in the Print What box and that the **Black & White** option and the **Scale to Fit Paper** option are selected.

❽ Click the **OK button** to print the overhead presentation. This completes the preparation of the presentation.

❾ Save your changes, then if you desire, you may exit PowerPoint.

Patricia is pleased with the appearance of her overhead masters. She asks her secretary to photocopy the transparency masters onto transparency sheets. Within a few days, Patricia receives her 35mm slides from Genigraphics Corporation. She is ready to give her presentation at the stockholders meeting.

DESIGN PRINCIPLE WINDOW

Giving an Effective Slide Show Presentation

- Dress appropriately for the meeting.
- Maintain a proper demeanor at all times.
- Introduce yourself and briefly explain what you'll be showing your audience.
- Look at your audience. Make adequate eye-to-eye contact.
- Speak clearly and audibly.
- If you're using a microphone, adjust it to your height so you won't have to lean down or stretch up to speak into it.
- Keep your language appropriate for the audience and situation. Avoid jargon, slang, and profanity.
- Summarize your presentation, come to a logical conclusion, and field questions courteously.

Questions

1. Define the following terms:
   a. background shade style
   b. variant (of a background shade style)
   c. transition effect
   d. build effect
   e. annotate a slide
2. Describe the purpose of the Slide Master and when you would use it.
3. List the advantages for creating a slide show beginning with a blank slide presentation rather than using the AutoContent Wizard.
4. Write a list of steps required to do the following:
   a. display the Slide Master
   b. change the background color and variant of a slide
   c. change the color scheme of a slide
   d. modify a bullet character and color
   e. insert slides from an existing presentation into the current presentation
   f. adding a transition effect to a slide
   g. add a build effect to a slide
5. What is the PowerPoint Viewer? When would you use it?
6. Describe how to get 35mm slides made from a PowerPoint slide presentation.
7. Describe what you would do to create overhead transparency masters from your PowerPoint slide presentation.

E 8. List one advantage and disadvantage of adding build effects with dimming of previous points to a slide containing bulleted items.

Tutorial Assignments

In the following Tutorial Assignment, make sure you click the Blank presentation button when you launch PowerPoint or, if PowerPoint is already running, click the New button on the Standard toolbar to create a new presentation. After working with a presentation and saving your changes, close the presentation.

Do the following:

1. Create a new blank presentation.
2. Create a title slide with the title "Employee Benefits" and the subtitle "Inca Imports International."
3. Using the Slide Master, change the color scheme to give a background color of dark blue-green (almost a forest green) and a text and line color of amber (orangish).
4. Change the shade style to From Corner, and the variant with the lightest color in the lower-left corner and the darkest in the upper-right corner.
5. Change the Master title style to a white Arial font.
6. In the Master main text, change the bullet color to red, but don't change the bullet character.
7. **E** In the second level text, change the text from black to Yellow #7 and the bullet from a dash to a red plus (+). *Hint*: From the Bullet dialog box, you can change the bullet to almost any color by clicking the down arrow under Special Color, then clicking Other Color to display the Other Color dialog box. When you click a color tile in the Other Color dialog box, the name of the color appears on the status bar.
8. Insert the Inca Imports logo (IIILOGO.BMP) into the Slide Master. Resize it to the approximate height of the Master title style text box. Position the logo in the lower-right corner of the text box of the Slide Master slide text style, near the text "Object Area for AutoLayouts."
9. **E** Return to Slide view and remove the Inca logo from the title slide. *Hint*: Use the same procedure you used when you removed the template diamond from the title slide in Tutorial 3.
10. Add a new slide with the Bulleted List AutoLayout.
11. Make the title of the new slide "Basic Benefits." Type the following first-level bulleted list items: "Medical and Dental Insurance," "Group Term Life Insurance," "Disability Insurance," "Occupational Accidental Death & Dismemberment Insurance," and "Master Retirement Plan."
12. Insert the existing presentation file T4FILE1.PPT into the current presentation.
13. In the new slide 3, demote the last two bulleted items, because they are the two types of supplemental retirement savings plans available to Inca Import employees.
14. **E** In slide 6, remove the bullets that appear to the left of the address of the benefits office. *Hint*: Display the Bullets menu, then deselect the checkbox labeled "Use a Bullet."
15. To all the slides, add the transition effect called "Random Transition."
16. To slides 2 through 5, add the build effect called "Blinds Horizontal." Select the Dim Previous Points option with gray as the dimmed color.
17. Run the slide show to ensure that the builds and transitions work properly.
18. Save the presentation as S4FILE3.PPT, then print the presentation in Black & White as handouts with four or six slides per page. Close the file.

Do the following:

19. Start a new blank presentation, and on the title slide, type the title "Employee of the Month," and the subtitle "Inca Imports International."
20. Using the Slide Master, change the color scheme to a background color of red and a text and line color of dark blue.
21. Select a background shade style Diagonal Right, and the variant with the lightest color in the upper-left corner and the darkest in the lower-right corner.
22. Change the Master title font size to 60-point Book Antiqua. If your computer doesn't have that font, use a different one.
23. Change the Master text styles so the font is 32-point Arial.
24. **E** Draw a large, red star in the middle of the Slide Master to serve as a backdrop for the slides in the presentation. *Hint*: Click the AutoShapes button in the Drawing toolbar, click the Star in the AutoShapes palette, press and hold down [Shift] while you drag from the upper left to the lower right of the slide. (Holding the [Shift] maintains the proportions of the image.) Center the star on the slide.

Change the slide color to Red #3 by clicking Format, clicking Colors and Lines, then selecting the desired color. (The color name appears on the status bar when you click a color tile in the Other Color dialog box.) Put the star behind the text by clicking Draw, then clicking Send to Back.

25. Near the upper-left corner of the Slide Master, insert the text "Employee of the Month." Make the text 24-point, white, Times New Roman (or a similar font).
E 26. Return to Slide view, and remove the Slide Master text and drawing from the title slide. *Hint*: Follow the procedure you used to remove the template diamond from the title slide in Tutorial 3.
27. Add a new slide with the Title Slide AutoLayout.
28. Make the title of the new slide "Alicia Cardon" and the subtitle "January."
29. Insert the existing presentation file T4FILE2.PPT into the current presentation.
E 30. To all the slides, add a transition effect and an automatic advance time, using the following method: In Slide Sort View, select all the slides, then click the Transition button on the Formatting toolbar to display the Transition dialog box. Change the Effect to "Cover Right." Set the speed to "Slow." In the Advance box, click Automatically After, then set the time to 4 seconds.
E 31. Set the slide show to run continuously. *Hint*: Click View, click Slide Show, click Use Slide Timings, and click Run Continuously Until 'Esc'.
32. Start the slide show and watch as the presentation automatically moves from one slide to the next and returns to the first slide after showing the last slide. If the slide show isn't automatic and continuous, you have made a mistake in one of the exercise items above. Review the steps and fix your mistake.
33. Press [Esc] to end the slide show after you've watched the entire presentation at least once.
34. Save the presentation as S4FILE4.PPT, then print the first three slides of the presentation in Black & White. Close the file.

Case Problems

1. Training on Sexual Harassment

Katherine Jaidar is the Director of Human Resources Development for McNeil Manufacturing Company, a large manufacturer of gardening supplies, like rakes, hoes, shovels, hoses, sprinkling systems, and tillers. One of her responsibilities is to provide training to McNeil employees on sexual harassment in the workplace. She prepares a PowerPoint slide presentation for her training classes as well as for a self-training presentation. Do the following:

1. Create a blank presentation with a title slide. Make the title "Sexual Harassment in the Workplace," the first line of the subtitle, "Training for employees of," and the second line of the subtitle " McNeil Manufacturing Company."
2. From the Slide Master, change the color scheme to give a background color of light blue and a text and line color of black.
3. Change the background shade style to Horizontal, and the variant with the darkest color on the left and lightest color on the right.
4. Change the Master title style to Arial font.
E 5. In the Master text style line (the first level in the bulleted list), change the bullet color to Yellow #8, but don't change the bullet style. *Hint*: The color name appears on the status bar when you click a color tile in the Other Color dialog box.
6. Return to Slide view, and add a new slide with the Bulleted List AutoLayout. Make the title "Definition of Sexual Harassment," and type the following bulleted items: "Promise of career enhancement for sexual favors," "Threats of career jeopardy if sexual demands are rejected," and "Deliberate, repeated, unsolicited comments, gestures, or physical actions of a sexual nature."

7. Insert the file P4HARAS.PPT after slide 2 of the current presentation.
8. On the new slide 3, reduce the size of the text box of the main text, and move the box down on the slide, so the slide appears more balanced top to bottom.
9. To each of the two slides with the titles "Don'ts" and "Do's," add an appropriate clip-art image.
10. Add "Fly from Bottom" build effects to all the slides that have bulleted lists. Include the feature to dim previous points using an appropriate color of your own choosing.

E 11. To all the slides, add the transition effect called "Checkerboard Across" with a slow speed. *Hint*: In Slide Sort View, select all the slides, then click the Transition button on the Formatting toolbar to display the Transition dialog box. Change the Effect to "Checkerboard Across" and set the speed to "Slow."

E 12. Check the spelling in your presentation. *Hint*: Begin by clicking Tools, then click Spelling.

13. Run the slide show to ensure that the builds and transitions work properly, save the presentation as S4HARAS.PPT, then print all the slides of the presentation in Black & White.

2. Report on Using a Presentation Graphics Program

You have agreed to give a presentation to a college fraternity on the benefits of using a presentation graphics program like PowerPoint. As you prepare your presentation using PowerPoint, use proper principles of planning and design as discussed throughout this book. Specifically do the following:

1. Create a blank presentation with a title slide. Choose your own title, but use your name as the subtitle.
2. From the Slide Master, change the background color to Violet #7, the shade style to Vertical, and the variant with the darkest color at the top and lightest color at the bottom.
3. Change the Master title style to Arial font of the color Blue #3, and change all the text in the Master text styles to the color white.
4. In the Master text style line (the first level in the bulleted list), change the bullet color to Yellow #8, but don't change the bullet character.
5. In the Slide Master, insert an appropriate clip art (such as a computer or a diskette). Make sure the clip-art image is simple enough so it can be seen clearly when reduced to a smaller size. Reduce the size so that the image is not more than about an inch in any dimension. Position the image in the lower-right corner of the text box of the Slide Master text style, near the text "Object Area for AutoLayouts."

E 6. Return to Slide view, and remove the graphic image from the title slide. *Hint*: Use the same procedure you used when you removed the template diamond from the title slide in Tutorial 3.

7. Add at least four new slides with the Bulleted List AutoLayout. For example, you might create a slide with the title "Advantages of Presentation Programs" and a list of advantages such as "Easy to use," "Easy to modify," "Professional quality," "Flexible," and so forth. Another example might be a title such as "Weaknesses of Presentation Programs" and a list of disadvantages such as "Requires expensive hardware," "Difficult to get appropriate clip art," "Requires extensive training," and so forth. Other possible titles include "Key Features of Presentation Software," "Possible Uses of Presentation Software," and "Steps in Learning How to use Presentation Software."
8. Add a slide with a graph so your audience can see a sample graph or chart. For example, the title might be "Cost of Presentation Software," with a bar graph

for the cost of PowerPoint, Harvard Graphics, WordPerfect Presentations, and Lotus Persuasion. If you can't easily obtain real numbers, make up some reasonable prices.

9. Add a summary slide with a bulleted list of the most important ideas in your presentation.
10. Add "Dissolve" build effects to all of the slides that have bulleted lists. Include the feature to dim previous points.
11. **E** To all the slides, add the transition effect called "Uncover Right-Down" with a slow speed. *Hint*: In Slide Sort View, select all the slides, then click the Transition button on the Formatting toolbar to display the Transition dialog box. Change the Effect to "Uncover Right-Down" and set the speed to "Slow."
12. Create speaker's notes for all of your slides. Include whatever information you need to help you with your presentation.
13. **E** Check the spelling in your presentation. *Hint*: Begin by clicking Tools, then clicking Spelling.
14. Run the slide show to ensure that the builds and transitions work properly.
15. Save the presentation as S4PRESNT.PPT, print all the slides of the presentation, and then print the speaker's notes in Black & White.
16. Create the file S4PRESNT.GNA that could be sent to Genigraphics for preparation of 35mm slides.
17. Use the Pick a Look Wizard to modify the presentation for creation of black-and-white overhead transparency masters.
18. Save the overhead version of the presentation as S4OVERHD.PPT, then print the overhead transparency masters.

3. Presentation on Personal Interest

Create a presentation on one of your personal interests, hobbies, or college courses. Your presentation might be on such topics as playing the piano, learning Spanish, astronomy, computer games, movies, horseback riding, physical fitness, dating, or cooking—anything that you're interested in and have some knowledge about. Do the following:

1. Choose an appropriate and attractive color scheme, background shading, and fonts. You may use the Pick a Look Wizard if you so desire.
2. Create a presentation of at least seven slides, including a title slide, at least three slides with bulleted lists, at least one slide with a graph or chart, a summary slide, and a blank slide (one with a black background) to signal the end of the presentation.
3. Add clip art or a drawing to the Slide Master.
4. Include speaker's notes on all the slides.
5. **E** Check the spelling of your presentation by clicking Tools, then clicking Spelling, and following the instructions on the Spelling dialog box.
6. Add transition effects for all slides. Add build effects (with dimming of previous points) for all slides with bulleted lists.
7. Save the presentation as S4HOBBY1.PPT, then print the slides as handouts (with 3 or 6 slides per page), and print the speaker's notes in Black & White.
8. Prepare the file S4HOBBY1.GNA for commercial preparation of 35mm slides by Genigraphics Corporation.

Index

G

H

I

L

M

N

O

P

Q

R

S

T

TASK REFERENCE

POWERPOINT 4.0 FOR WINDOWS

Italicized page numbers indicate the first discussion of each task.

TASK	MOUSE	MENU	KEYBOARD
Add a coworker to an organizational chart, PP 70	Click Co-worker:, click existing box		
Add build effects, PP 98	Click	In Slide Sorter view, click Tools, click Build	
Add subordinate levels to an organizational chart, PP 69	Click Subordinate:, click existing box		
Add transition effects, PP 96	Click	In Slide Sorter view, click Tools, click Transition	
Annotate a slide, PP 100	In Slide Show view, click		
AutoContent Wizard, PP 27	Click, then click AutoContent Wizard	Click File, click New, then click AutoContent Wizard	
Bold text, PP 43	Click B	Click Format, click Font, click Bold, click the OK button	Ctrl B
Center paragraph	Click	Click Format, click Alignment, click Center	Ctrl E
Change background color, PP 88		Click Format, click Slide Background, click Change Color, click the color, click the OK button, click Apply or Apply to All	
Change bullet, PP 89		Click Format, click Bullet, select the bullet character and color, click the OK button	
Change slide layout, PP 60		Click Format, click Slide Layout	
Change slide color scheme, PP 86		Click Format, click Slide Color Scheme	
Change text font, PP 43	Click next to font, click font	Click Format, click Font, click the font, click the OK button	Ctrl Shift F
Change text point size, PP 43	Click next to font size, click size	Click Format, click Font, click the font size, click the OK button	Ctrl Shift P
Change Text Color, PP 44	Click	Click Format, click Font, change the color, click the OK button	
Check Spelling, PP 49	Click	Click Tools, click Spelling	F7 or Alt Ctrl L
Close		Click File, click Close	Ctrl W or Ctrl F4
Copy	Select text, click	Select text, click Edit, click Copy	Ctrl C

TASK REFERENCE

POWERPOINT 4.0 FOR WINDOWS

Italicized page numbers indicate the first discussion of each task.

TASK	MOUSE	MENU	KEYBOARD
Cut, PP 37	Select text, click	Select text, click Edit, click Cut	Ctrl X
Date		Go to Slide Master, click Insert, click Date	Alt Shift D
Decrease text font size	Click		Ctrl Shift <
Delete character right, PP 32			Del
Delete character left, PP 32			Backspace
Delete slide, PP 36		In Slide Sorter or Outline view, select slide, click Edit, click Delete Slide	Del
Delete word left			Ctrl Backspace
Delete word right			Ctrl Del
Demote paragraph, PP 34	Click		Alt Shift →
Draw a shape, PP 71	Click , click the desired shape, drag the mouse on the slide		
Exit/Quit, PP 22		Click File, click Exit	Ctrl Q or Alt F4
Find		Click Edit, click Find	Ctrl F
Flip an object, PP 72		Click Draw, click Rotate/Flip, click Flip Vertical or Flip Horizontal	
Group		Select objects, click Draw, click Group	Ctrl Shift G
Help, Contents, PP 20		Click Help, click Contents	F1
Help, Search, PP 21		Click Help, click Search for Help on	
Increase text font size	Click		Ctrl Shift >
Insert a title into a graph, PP 66		Click Insert, click Titles	
Insert a picture, PP 58		Click Insert, click Picture	
Insert clip art, PP 62	Click	Click Insert, click Clip Art	
Insert a graph, PP 65	Click	Click Insert, click Object, click Microsoft Graph	
Insert an organizational chart, PP 68	Click	Click Insert, click Object, click Microsoft Organizational Chart	
Insert slides from a disk file, PP 93		Click Insert, click Slides from File	

TASK REFERENCE

POWERPOINT 4.0 FOR WINDOWS

Italicized page numbers indicate the first discussion of each task.

TASK	MOUSE	MENU	KEYBOARD
Italicize text, PP 43	Click	Click Format, click Font, click Italic, click the OK button	Ctrl I
Justify paragraph		Click Format, click Alignment, click Justify	Ctrl J
Left-align paragraph, PP 57	Click	Click Format, click Alignment, click Left	Ctrl L
Make text plain		Click Format, click Font, click Regular, click the OK button	Ctrl Shift Z
Move selected paragraph up, PP 34	Click		Alt Shift ↑
Move selected paragraph down, PP 34	Click		Alt Shift ↓
New presentation	Click	Click File, click New	Ctrl N
New slide, PP 40	Click	Click Insert, click New Slide	Ctrl M
Next slide, PP 18	Click		PgDn
Notes Page View, PP 17	Click	Click View, click Notes Pages	
Open, PP 8	Click	Click File, click Open	Ctrl O
Outline View, PP 16	Click	Click View, click Outline	Alt Ctrl O
Paste, PP 37	Click	Click Edit, click Paste	Ctrl V
Pick a Look Wizard, PP 27	Click	Click Format, click Pick a Look Wizard	
Prepare 35mm slides, PP 103		Click File, click Slide Setup, select Slides Sized for 35mm Slide, click the OK button, click File, click Print, Genigraphics Driver on GENI, follow instructions in dialog boxes	
Previous slide, PP 11	Click		PgUp
Print, PP 19	Click	Click File, click Print	Ctrl P or Ctrl Shift F12
Promote paragraph, PP 34	Click		Alt Shift ←
Replace		Click Edit, click Replace	Ctrl H
Right-align paragraph		Click Format, click Alignment, click Right	Ctrl R
Rotate an object, PP 74	Click	Click Draw, click Rotate/Flip, click Free Rotate, drag a resize handle	

TASK REFERENCE

POWERPOINT 4.0 FOR WINDOWS

Italicized page numbers indicate the first discussion of each task.

TASK	MOUSE	MENU	KEYBOARD
Save, PP 19	Click [Save button]	Click File, click Save	Ctrl S or Shift F12
Save As, PP 10		Click File, click Save As	F12
Show all text and headings, PP 30	Click [Show All button]		Alt Shift A
Show titles, PP 30	Click [Show Titles button]		Alt Shift 1
Slide Master view, PP 85	Hold down Shift and click [Slide View button]		
Slide Show View	Click [Slide Show button]	Click View, click Slide Show, click Show	
Slide Sorter View, PP 12	Click [Slide Sorter button]	Click View, click Slide Sorter	Alt Ctrl P
Slide View, PP 37	Click [Slide View button]	Click View, click Slides	Alt Ctrl N
Underline text, PP 43	Click [Underline button]	Click Format, click Font, click Underline, click the OK button	Ctrl U
Undo	Click [Undo button]	Click Edit, click Undo	Ctrl Z
Ungroup, PP 64		Select object, click Draw, click Ungroup	Ctrl Shift H